THE BUSINESS OF SCHOLARLY PUBLISHING

THE BUSINESS OF SCHOLARLY PUBLISHING

Managing in Turbulent Times

Albert N. Greco

OXFORD
UNIVERSITY PRESS

OXFORD
UNIVERSITY PRESS

Oxford University Press is a department of the University of Oxford. It furthers the University's objective of excellence in research, scholarship, and education by publishing worldwide. Oxford is a registered trade mark of Oxford University Press in the UK and certain other countries.

Published in the United States of America by Oxford University Press
198 Madison Avenue, New York, NY 10016, United States of America.

Library of Congress Cataloging-in-Publication Data
Names: Greco, Albert N., 1945– author.
Title: The business of scholarly publishing : managing in turbulent times /
Albert N. Greco, Fordham University.
Description: New York, NY : Oxford University Press, [2020] |
Includes bibliographical references and index.
Identifiers: LCCN 2019044739 (print) | LCCN 2019044740 (ebook) |
ISBN 9780190626235 (hardback) | ISBN 9780190626259 (epub) |
ISBN 9780190626266 (online)
Subjects: LCSH: Scholarly publishing—United States.
Classification: LCC Z480.S37 G74 2020 (print) | LCC Z480.S37 (ebook) |
DDC 070.5—dc23
LC record available at https://lccn.loc.gov/2019044739
LC ebook record available at https://lccn.loc.gov/2019044740

The manufacturer's authorised representative in the EU for product safety is Oxford University Press España S.A. of El Parque Empresarial San Fernando de Henares, Avenida de Castilla, 2 – 28830 Madrid (www.oup.es/en or product.safety@oup.com). OUP España S.A. also acts as importer into Spain of products made by the manufacturer.

For Elaine

CONTENTS

PREFACE

To understand the business of scholarly journal and book publishing, a number of statistical sources from various US government departments and agencies, as well as nongovernment sources including US and foreign trade associations, were utilized in this book.

However, there is an inevitable lag in obtaining reliable datasets from governmental sources. In addition, some governmental agencies, and a few industry associations, released preliminary totals or estimates for certain years (e.g., 2013–2016). In addition, various sources rounded off certain tallies, which means that not all percentages always equal 100%.

Therefore, the best available datasets as of February 2019 were utilized in this book.

ACKNOWLEDGMENTS

I want to thank everyone for their assistance in the development of this book.

James Cook, an expert editor at Oxford University Press, for all of his assistance during the writing and editing of this book; and Macey Fairchild, at Oxford University Press, for her help in the editorial review and the production of this book.

The numerous discussions about the eclectic book publishing industry with my sons, Al, Tim, John, and Robert. I must also acknowledge the support of my daughters-in-law, Teresa, Gee, Michele, and Sandy. Of course, I cannot forget my grandchildren, Gabrielle, Olivia, Nicolette, James, Gianna, Liam, Rosie, Annabelle, Julian, and Francis, in what has been a long but exceptionally interesting journey to complete this book.

Lastly, I had a number of very useful conversations about scholarly publishing with Alex Holzman and, since 1985, with members of the university press and commercial scholarly publishing communities, including John Tebbel, Linda Bathgate, and Tom Radko.

[1]

THE CHANGING ENVIRONMENT FOR SCHOLARLY PUBLISHING

The importance of the publishing and dissemination of scholarly books and journals remains secure since this process is pivotal to the life blood of academic research. However, the process of scholarly publishing and dissemination in the United States has undergone a series of major substantive developments that have, in many instances, improved the quality and dissemination of content and, in a few cases, impacted negatively on this ecosystem. These substantive developments include the following.

AN INCREASE IN THE NUMBER OF COLLEGES IN THE UNITED STATES AND THE RELATED GROWTH IN THE NUMBER OF FACULTY MEMBERS AND ACADEMIC LIBRARIES

In 1940, there were 1,708 colleges and universities in the United States, and these institutions of higher learning had 1,494,203 students and an instructional staff (i.e., faculty members) of 110,885.[1] By 2015, the last year actual and not projected data was available from the US Department of Education (Education), the number of colleges and universities topped 4,583 (+168.33% since 1940) with 19,977,000 students (+1,236.97%) and 1,561,000 faculty members (+1,307.76%).[2]

This period of phenomenal growth since 1940, the last year before the entry of the United States into World War II, triggered a sharp increase in the number of academic libraries and the need for scholarly content.[3] As more institutions were created and branch colleges launched, many college and university administrators (i.e., presidents, provosts, deans, and department chairs) began to reevaluate the terms and conditions related to hiring decisions as well as tenure and promotion policies. At many institutions, this led to the creation of relatively rigid "publish or perish" procedures.

THE DEVELOPMENT OF "PUBLISH OR PERISH" PROCEDURES AT MANY US COLLEGES AND THE PURSUIT OF PRESTIGE AT THESE INSTITUTIONS OF HIGHER LEARNING

"Publish or perish" procedures are the modern-day version of the "Sword of Damocles" hanging over the head of every recent doctoral graduate who wants an academic appointment, every faculty member who wants tenure and a promotion, and every researcher who needs funding to conduct an experiment. While many scholars have insisted that publishing contributes significantly to teaching and research, others have criticized the system for perpetuating the publication of far too many "useless" or "questionable" research studies.[4] The dominant strategy at most universities today is unquestionably to acquire prestige based, to a degree, on scholarly output in major journals or books published by prestigious university presses and commercial scholarly publishers.[5] In essence, many components of higher education in the United States adopted the mantra of Hollywood that "too much is never enough."

Unfortunately, at some institutions this was done at the expense of undergraduate and graduate instruction.[6] For good or bad, the imprints of certain publishers in certain fields provided the prestige and the means for universities to separate quality from quantity.[7]

CONSOLIDATION IN THE SCHOLARLY PUBLISHING INDUSTRY: THE QUEST FOR SCALE

Regardless of one's opinion about the intrinsic merits of the "publish or perish" philosophy, scholarly publishing matters. Without the dissemination of scholarly content, scholarship is imperiled because academics and researchers rely on the positive and negative responses of readers and critics to improve their methodology, correct errors, etc. And this has been the case for about 541 years.

The major developments in the modern history of scholarly communications include the invention of the modern printing press and moveable type by Gutenberg (about 1450), the creation of a scholarly printing operation at the Sorbonne (1470), printing endeavors at Oxford (1478), the launching of a press at Cambridge (1586), and the establishing of viable scholarly journals in France and England (1665).[8]

While European centers of learning dominated the publication and dissemination of scholarly content for several centuries, a series of developments in the United States played a major role in the creation of a viable scholarly publishing ecosystem.

First, the creation of land-grant universities in the years after 1862 triggered the creation of major state-supported universities. Second, certain US colleges and universities accepted the well-respected German university graduate school model emphasizing research publications.[9] Third, electricity allowed printing presses to produce scholarly books and journals quickly and efficiently. Fourth, the creation of a viable transcontinental transportation system allowed the rapid distribution of content. Fifth, the US Congress's 1944 landmark Servicemen's Readjustment Act (also known as the GI Bill of Rights) provided governmental funding for a variety of educational options for returning veterans including skilled trade schools, colleges, and graduate schools. Sixth, there was phenomenal growth in the number of junior/community colleges, four-year colleges, and graduate and professional schools after the end of World War II.[10]

Many of these events and developments enabled certain universities to launch university presses in the late 19th and early 20th centuries.[11] While many of these university presses were originally small and generally had thinly staffed operations, by the 21st century, there were world-class university presses throughout the United States, Canada, Europe, Asia, the Pacific Rim, Africa, and the Middle East.[12]

Another important development was the creation of academic societies that supported regional and national conferences and developed impressive scholarly publishing operations. Some of the more prominent societies include the American Antiquarian Society (1812), the American Economic Association (1885), the American Philosophical Society (1743), the American Chemical Society (1876), and the American Mathematical Society (1888). Clearly, before and immediately after the end of World War II, academic publishing was dominated by a rather small number of university presses and professional societies.[13]

After the end of World War II, many economists began to write about the importance of scale,[14] and this triggered a reevaluation of some of the classic economic articles and theories on this topic by Adam Smith, Alfred Marshall, and John Maynard Keynes.[15] By the 1950s and 1960s, the "conglomerate phenomenon" emerged with tremendous publicity as more commercial scholarly publishing companies accepted the premises of modern portfolio theory, devised by Harry Markowitz,[16] and they began to diversify into related and, in many instances, unrelated industries. While scholars investigated the theory and impact of diversification and conglomerates on mergers and acquisitions,[17] concerns emerged about some negative issues, specifically "predatory" acquisitions.[18]

It was perhaps inevitable that companies began to evaluate acquisitions in the publishing sector to expand operations and harness the potential of scale in the acquisition, production, and dissemination of content.[19] Many of these companies (e.g., RELX, Wolters Kluwer, John Wiley, Informa, and Springer Nature) were able to utilize the positive features of scale to increase the number of scholarly books and scholarly journals, to create new books and journals addressing important subcategories (i.e., the impact of "twigging" in scholarly publishing), and to launch online platforms that made access to content relatively easy.

However, critics of the growth of the scholarly companies complained that an "oligopoly" was created[20] that drove up the price of books[21] and especially journals at a time when academic and research libraries were underfunded or unable to handle effectively the movement toward digital products.[22] This situation compelled many academic and research libraries to curtail the purchase of books to meet the demand for journals (known as the "serials crisis").[23]

Some scholars believed that viable open access (OA) journals launched and sustained by charging an author an article processing charge (APC) might ameliorate the increases in journal subscriptions. In essence, the author pays, and the journal article is free to the library or to any reader. In theory, APCs could be paid from a researcher's grant, a university, a school, an academic department, or the library, relieving the library from paying costly journal subscriptions. While this approach generated a significant amount of attention and support within certain academic and library circles, APCs remain an intriguing theory since APCs alone cannot support the entire scholarly journal publishing system.

The OA options included (1) green OA journal (i.e., posting an article for no fee on a website maintained by the author, a university, or an organization); (2) a gold OA journal (a journal that charged an APC; APCs can vary significantly from less than $100 to +$5,000);[24]

(3) a diamond OA that does not charge any APC and is free for anyone to access, and all costs are paid for by a society (perhaps the American Marketing Association), an institution (perhaps a university or an academic department), or a funding agency (perhaps the Bill and Melinda Gates Foundation); (4) the creation of "mega-journals" (e.g., *BMC Notes*) and hybrid journals (i.e., journals offering authors the option of submitting an article for no fee and transferring the copyright to the publisher, or submitting the article when accepted for publication for an APC, allowing free access to the article;[25] and (5) institutional repositories (IRs). All of these options relied on the electronic dissemination of content.[26]

REDUCTION IN THE NUMBER OF BOOKSTORES AND THE EMERGENCE OF ONLINE BOOK RETAILERS

A series of major events transformed the selling of books in the United States. In 1994 there were 28,137 brick-and-mortar bookstores in the United States, and the majority were independent stores.[27] Total annual bookstore revenues stood at $10.107 billion.[28] This retail landscape changed with the development of large national bookstore chains (e.g., Barnes & Noble, Borders, Crown Books, Books-a-Million) and a cluster of smaller regional independent chains (e.g., Tattered Cover). Amazon.com was launched in July 1995.[29]

By 2018 there were approximately 13,928 brick-and-mortar bookstores (–50.5% since 1994)[30] generating annual sales of $10.729 billion (+6.15%).[31] To put bookstore revenue into perspective, the cumulative inflation rate between 1994 and 2017 was 65.18%.[32] If bookstore revenue kept pace with inflation, $10.107 billion in 1994 should have been +$16.7 billion in 2018.

The large national chains negatively impacted many independent bookstores, and the net result was a loss of more than 14,000 bookstores in the United States, a draconian decline in the number of bookstores and bookshelves stocking titles, including academic books, that enabled readers to discover books. The movement toward ordering books from online websites selling new and used books also transformed the scholarly book publishing industry, now dependent to a significant degree on an online site listing and stocking a new scholarly book. While online access provides an individual with "frictionless" commercial opportunities, the ability to move easily and quickly from one website to another, discovery of a new or used title is not always as easy, or as pleasant, as in a bookstore. In any case, the sale of scholarly books in the United States has been transformed for academics and "general readers."

MOST SCHOLARLY PUBLISHERS ARE TRYING TO DEFEND THEIR EXISTING MARKET SHARE: SOME STRATEGIES WORK AND SOME DO NOT

Scholarly publishing is not a declining industry; it is an industry in transition from one that was 100% print, a hybrid one that offers content in both print and digital formats, and a complete 100% OA digital model. The increase in the number of scholarly journals and books indicates clearly that there is a need, and a dramatic need, to publish and disseminate important research in the humanities, the social sciences, and the eclectic science, technology, and medical fields. Scholarly publishing is a mature industry that has existed for over 100 years in the United States and goes back over 541 years in the United Kingdom and parts of Europe, an issue discussed in an important article by Peter J. Dougherty (the former director at Princeton University Press).[33]

Most university presses rely extensively on subsidies from their university, and societies support their scholarly journals and books. Regrettably, most university presses lack scale (witness the recent closing of the University Press of New England),[34] and most learned societies rely on income from regional or national meetings and the sale of publications.

Many academic and research libraries have seen their budgets stagnate during years of sharp increases in expenses in the last 25 years.[35] This prompted many libraries to launch IR to combat what they viewed as the pernicious increases in the prices of various scholarly products.[36]

EMPLOYMENT IN ACADEMIC PUBLISHING

Who works at scholarly publishing firms? Has scholarly publishing been impacted negatively by discriminatory practices? The published literature about university presses, learned societies, and commercial scholarly publishers is unquestionably extensive, with several journals and countless articles and books addressing the managerial or marketing successes or failures of this large industry. Yet very little research has been conducted about the people who make up the scholarly publishing ecosystem and if any discriminatory policies were evident.

One study, conducted in late 2014 and early 2015, was an international survey of approximately 6,121 scholarly publishing employees in 33 nations. The results indicated that while a large percentage of employees were females, few held major managerial positions, and the clear majority were Caucasians.[37] The only study of gender disparity in the publication of humanities books was conducted in the summer and fall of 2016. Researchers collected, aggregated, and analyzed data on 1,633 faculty members, at the top 50 US English-language and literature academics departments, who authored or edited 4,835 scholarly books. The findings were rather revealing. Women accounted for more than 60% of all the PhD degrees in English language and literature since 1987. Yet these top 50 departments have more male than female faculty members, and male faculty members publish more scholarly books on a per capita basis.[38] Only two articles have appeared on these subjects, and additional research is clearly needed.

THE IMPORTANCE OF COPYRIGHT PROTECTION TO THE SCHOLARLY PUBLISHING COMMUNITY

Copyright protection is the fuel that keeps the scholarly publishing "engine" fully operational. Ironically, both the Declaration of Independence and the Constitution of the United States are silent regarding copyright and intellectual property issues. However, the Constitution in Article 1 §8 lists in some detail the powers of the Congress of the United States.[39] "The Congress shall have Power To lay and collect Taxes, Duties, Imposts and Excises, to pay the Debts and provide for the common Defense and general Welfare of the United States . . . To promote the Progress of Science and useful Arts, by securing for limited Times to Authors and Inventors the exclusive Right to their respective Writings and Discoveries."[40]

Clearly, this section grants Congress the authorization to create laws regarding copyrights and other issues. It was then up to Congress to draft a copyright law. In 1790 the first US copyright law was passed, and it stipulated the following: (1) that copyright protection would be for 14 years, with a renewal for another 14 years; (2) a description of and penalties for copyright infringement; (3) deposit requirements; (4) importing or "vending" any copyrighted work in the United States; and (5) suing or prosecuting a copyright infringer.[41]

The 1790 law remained in effect until a series of substantive revisions were passed by the Congress: (1) the Copyright Act of 1831 extended copyright protection to 28 years, with the possibility of an additional 14-years;[42] (2) the Copyright Act of 1870 included the centralization of all copyright activities within the Library of Congress, registration and deposit requirements, and a realization that works of art and derivative works required protection under US copyright law;[43] and (3) the Copyright Act of 1909 extended the copyright term to 56 years, broadened the subject matter of copyright protection, and clarified various vexing dating procedures.[44]

No important change in the copyright law took place between 1909 and 1946 because of the impact of World War I, the Great Depression, and World War II. However, in 1947 Congress made an incredibly important change to the copyright system. Congress codified the entire US copyright law into one rather long and ultimately complex document, known as 17 U.S.C.[45]

In 1976, Congress passed the most comprehensive copyright law in the nation's history. The important changes included the following: (1) the term of copyright protection was extended to the life of the author and 50 years after the death of the author; (2) a copyright held by a corporation (e.g., the Walt Disney Company) was extended to 75 years; (3) the law preempted any existing state copyright laws, an interesting change since state laws were clearly subservient to federal laws under the terms of Article VI clause 2 of the US Constitution, known as the "supremacy clause"; (4) all works published before January 1, 1978, had a copyright renewal term of 47 years, for a total of 75 years; (5) the scope and subjected matter of copyrighted works was broadened; and (6) copyright infringements, fair use, and copyright defenses and remedies were also resolved. These provisions brought US copyright law into compliance with the Berne Convention for the Protection of Literary and Artistic Works.[46]

While the 1976 changes were of great importance, Congress modified the copyright law in 1998 in the Copyright Term Extension Act of 1998.[47] The key provisions included the following: (1) the term of copyright protection was extended to the life of the author and 70 years after the death of the author; (2) all corporate copyrights were extended to 120 years after the creation of the work or 95 years after the work's original publication—this provision has been called the "Mickey Mouse" clause because of its continued protection of the cartoon character Mickey Mouse; and (3) all works published prior to January 1, 1978, were extended to 95 years—this clause meant that certain important literary and historical works published in the 1920s would start to fall out of copyright protection in the years after 2020.[48] In addition, Congress passed the 1998 Digital Millennium Copyright Act, which included language concerning violations of digital rights management systems and procedures and copyright infringement on the Internet.[49]

Since 1998, Congress has not passed any revisions to these copyright laws, an issue of concern to certain members of the intellectual property community in light of the development of the Internet, laptops and tablets, the digital posting of content, etc.

FINAL OBSERVATIONS ON THE STATE OF SCHOLARLY PUBLISHING

First, scholarly publishing is a business; it is not a social service. The managers of scholarly publishing books and journals, whether at university presses, academic societies, or commercial academic presses, have a fiduciary responsibility to either their university, society members, or stockholders to handle carefully and professionally the assets they have been entrusted with by the "owners" of these assets. While this fact is well known in business and legal circles, it appears, after reviewing the published literature, that some academics and researchers failed to understand this rather basic legal point.

Second, in light of the perplexing economic and business developments since 1980, including five recessions that lasted a total of 56 months,[50] most scholarly publishers must modify their basic business model and acquire scale. And in the case of university presses, learned societies, and libraries involved in publishing activities, they must demonstrate convincingly to their home institutions, their authors, and their customers their nonmonetary social value and worth. Small- to medium-sized commercial scholarly presses must satisfy boards and stockholders that they have value, and that they should remain viable, independent scholarly publishing entities. Otherwise, the future of many of these important scholarly publishing operations will be in peril, and scholarship itself would be in jeopardy.

In the following chapters, some of the strategies and structures that were adopted successfully by scholarly publishing operations will be analyzed, including evaluations of the threats of new market entrants, supplier power, competitive rivalries, buyer power, and product and technology development issues. Other substantive issues that will be scrutinized include strategies related to cost leadership and differentiation, economic and financial issues, and distribution matters. Unfortunately, some strategies proved to be unsuccessful, triggering setbacks in the marketplace.

While this book covers the period since the end of World War II, it focuses primarily on the years since 2000, which have seen almost revolutionary changes in markets, technology, library and individual purchasing patterns, and funding within the scholarly publishing ecosystem, including the acceptance of big data and predictive analytics.[51] As with all ecosystems, individual species (i.e., scholarly publishing operations) are evolving to survive; however, as with all ecosystems, not all will succeed, and new species will appear.

NOTES

1. US Department of Education, Office of Educational Research and Improvement, "120 Years of American Education: A Statistical Portrait," Table 23: Historical Summary of Higher Education Statistics: 1869–1990, https://nces.ed.gov/pubs93/93442.pdf.
2. US Department of Education, National Center for Education Statistics, "Projections of Education Statistics to 2022," Table 20: Actual and Projected Numbers for Total Enrolment in All Postsecondary-Granting Institutions," https//nces.ed.gov/pubs2014/2014051.pdf.
3. Albert N. Greco, "Academic Libraries and the Economics of Scholarly Publishing in the Twentieth-First Century: Portfolio Theory, Product Differentiation, Economic Rent, Perfect Price Discrimination, and the Cost of Prestige," *Journal of Scholarly Publishing* 47, 1 (October 2015):

1–43. Also see Aileen Fyfe, Kelly Coate, Stephen Curry, Stuart Lawson, Noah Moxham, and Camilla Mork Rostvik, "Untangling Academic Publishing: A History of the Relationship Between Commercial Interests, Academic Prestige, and the Circulation of Research," https://doi.org/10.5281/zenodo.546100.

4. Emily Conover, "There Are Too Many Scientific Studies, New Study Reports," https://www.sciencemag.org/news/2015/03/there-are-too-many-scientific-studies-new-study-reports; and Pietro Della Briotta Parolo, Raj Kumar Pan, Rumi Ghosh, Bernardo A. Huberman, Kimmo Kaski, and Santo Fortunato, "Attention Decay in Science," arXiv:1503.01881v1.pdf. Also see Vincent Lariviere and Rodigo Costas, "How Many Is Too Many? On the Relationship Between Research Productivity and Impact," *PloS One* 11, 9 (September 28, 1016), doi:10.1371/journal.pone_0162709; Charlotte Price Person and Johanne Uhrenholt Kusnitzoff, "Crisis in Basic Research: Scientists Publish Too Much," https://sciencenordic.com/academia-basic-research-basic-research-crisis-in-in-research-scientists-publish-too-much/1442296; Leslie K. John, George Loewenstein, and Drazen Prejec, "Measuring the Prevalence of Questionable Research Practices With Incentives for Truth Telling," *Psychological Science* 23, 5 (2012): 524–532; Timo Hannay, "Stop the Deluge of Science Research," *The Guardian*, https://www.theguardian.com/higher-education-network/blog/2014/aug/05/why-we-should-publish-less-scientific-research; Dahlia Remier, "Are 90% of Academic Papers Really Never Cited? Reviewing the Literature on Academic Citations," https://blogs.lse.ac.uk/impactofsocialsciences/2014/04/23/academic-papers-citation-rates-remier; Christopher Schaberg, "Publish or Perish? Yes. Embrace It," *Chronicle of Higher Education,* February 15, 2016, https://www.chronicle.com/article/Publish-or-Perish-Yes/235319; Alison Smith, "Publish or Perish: The Write Thing for Nursing," *Nursing Economics* 22, 6 (November/December 2004): 342–343; Natalia Herraiz, "Publish or Perish in Spain," *Foreign Policy* 150 (September/October 2005): 104.

5. James E. Richard, Geoff Plimmer, Kim-Shyan Fem, and Charles Campbell, "Publishing Success of Marketing Academics: Antecedents and Outcomes," *European Journal of Marketing* 49, 1/2 (2015): 123–145. Mark de Rond and Alan N. Miller, "Publish or Perish: Bane or Boon of Academic Life?," *Journal of Management Inquiry* 14, 4 (December 2005): 321–329.

6. Jameel Hasan, "AACSB's Benign Neglect of Faculty Teaching Effectiveness and Excessive Emphasis on Research Productivity: Profess or Perish vs. Publish or Perish," *Academy of Business Journal* 1, 1 (2016): 29–45.

7. Colin Eden and Sue Jones, "Publish or Perish? A Case Study," *Journal of Operational Research Society* 32, 2 (February 1980): 131–139.
8. Albert N. Greco, "The Impact of Disruptive Technologies on Scholarly Journals," *Journal of Scholarly Publishing* 48, 1 (October 2016): 17–39.
9. Cecile M. Jagodzinski, "The University Press in North America: A Brief History," *Journal of Scholarly Publishing* 40, 1 (October 2008): 1–20.
10. Michael Lind, *Land of Promise: An Economic History of the United States* (New York: HarperCollins, 2013), 81–131, 187–213.
11. Sue Ann Gardner, "Scholarly Publishing in the U.S., Then and Now: A Brief History and Implications for the Future," University of Nebraska Lincoln, Digital Commons@University of Nebraska-Lincoln, 2012, http://digitalcommons.unl.edu/library_talks/81. Richard Abel, "The National Enquiry Into Scholarly Communication—Twenty Years After," *Publishing Research Quarterly* 15, 1 (Spring 1999): 3–19.
12. August Fruge, *A Skeptic Among Scholars* (Berkeley: University of California Press, 1993), 7–36. Also see Lewis A. Coser, Charles Kadushin, and Walter W. Powell, *Books: The Culture and Commerce of Publishing* (Chicago: University of Chicago Press, 1983), 13–35. Albert Henderson, "The Growth of Printed Literature in the Twentieth Century," in *Scholarly Publishing: Books, Journals, Publishers, and Libraries in the Twentieth Century*, ed. Richard L. Abel, Lyman W. Newlin, and Katrina Strauch (New York: John Wiley & Sons, 2002), 1–24.
13. Gardner, "Scholarly Publishing in the U.S., Then and Now: A Brief History and Implications for the Future," University of Nebraska Lincoln, Digital Commons@University of Nebraska- Lincoln, 2012, http://digitalcommons.unl.edu/library_talks/81.
14. Ronald E. Seavoy, *An Economic History of the United States From 1607 to the Present* (New York: Routledge, 2006), 121–239.
15. Aubrey Silberston, "Economies of Scale in Theory and Practice," *Economic Journal* 82, 325 (March 1972): 369–391. Also see Adam Smith, *The Wealth of Nations* (New York: Bantam Books, 2003), book 1, chapter 1, pp. 8–9; book 1, chapter 7, p. 69; book 1, chapter 10, p. 136; book 4, introduction, p. 459; book 4, chapter 2, pp. 488–489; book 4, chapter 7, part 3, p. 667; book 4, chapter 1, part 2, p. 775. Alfred Marshall, *Principles of Economics* (New York: Palgrave Macmillan, 2013), 54–60, 63–66, 86–91, 92–100, 124–130, 153–169. John Maynard Keynes, *The General Theory of Employment, Interest, and Money* (New York: BN Publishing, 2008), 13–32, 37–40, 88–94, 161–162, 163–176, 177–184, 185–195.
16. Harry Markowitz, "Portfolio Selection," *Journal of Finance* 7, 1 (March 1952): 77–91. Also see Markowitz, "Foundations of Portfolio Theory," *Journal of Finance* 46, 2 (June 1991): 469–477.

17. Timothy M. Hurley, "The Urge to Merge: Contemporary Theories on the Rise of Conglomerate Mergers in the 1960s," *Journal of Business & Technology Law* 1, 1 (2006): 185–205. Also see Heim Levy and Marshall Sarnat, "Diversification, Portfolio Analysis, and the Uneasy Case for Conglomerate Mergers," *Journal of Finance* 25 (1970): 795–802. Gerald F. Davis, Kristina A. Diekmann, and Catherine H. Tinsley, "The Decline and Fall of the Conglomerate Firm in the 1980s: The Deinstitutionalization of an Organizational Ford," *American Sociological Review* 59 (August 1994): 547–570. Francesco Guerrera, "Decline Sets In at the Conglomerate," *Financial Times,* February 6, 2007, https://www.ft.com/content// 58d234fb48c-11db-b707-0000779e2340.
18. Brad M. Barber, Donald Palmer, and James Wallace, "Determinants of Conglomerate and Predatory Acquisitions: Evidence From the 1960s," *Journal of Corporate Finance* 1, 3–4 (April 1995): 283–318. Also see Gerald F. Davis and Suzanne K. Stout, "Organization Theory and the Market for Corporate Control: A Dynamic Analysis of the Characteristics of Large Takeover Targets, 1980–1990," *Administrative Science Quarterly* 37 (1992): 605–633.
19. Reece McGee, "The Economics of Conglomerate Organization," *Society* 17, 1 (September 1979): 42–47. Also see Hal R. Mason and Maurice Goudzwaard, "Performance of Conglomerate Firms: A Portfolio Approach," *Journal of Finance* 31 (1976): 39–48. Michael C. Jensen and William H. Meckling, "Theory of the Firm: Managerial Behavior, Agency Cost, and Ownership Structure," *Journal of Financial Economics* 3 (1976): 305–360.
20. Vincent Lariviere, Stefanie Haustein, and Philippe Mongeon, "The Oligopoly of Academic Publishers in the Digital Era," *PLoS One* 100, 6 (June 10, 2015): e0127502. doi:10.1371/journal.pone.0127502. Also see Alejandro Posada and George Chen, "Preliminary Findings: Rent Seeking by Elsevier: Publishers Are Increasingly in Control of Scholarly Infrastructure and Why We Should Care," Knowledge Gap, 1–11, http://knowledge gap.org/index.php/sub-projects/rent-seeking-and financialization-of-the-academic-publishing-industry/preliminary-findings. David R. Scott and Nicole Eva, "The Canadian Dollar Versus the Collection: How Canadian University Libraries Are Coping," *Canadian Journal of Library and Information Practice and Research* 11, 2: 1–4, https://journal.lib.uoguelph.ca/index.pho/perj/article/view/ 3771#.Wpco6Grwa.JB. Adriane MacDonald and Nicole Eva, "It's Time to Stand Up to the Academic Publishing Industry," University Affairs, https://www.universityaffairs.ca/opinion/in-my-opinion/time-stand-academic-publishing industry. Stephen Curry, "It's Time for Academics to Take Back Control of Research Journals," *The Guardian*, 1–4, https://

www.theguardian.com/higher-education-network/2017/may/25/its-time-for-academics-to-take-bck-control-of-research-journals. Casey Brienza, "Opening the Wrong Gate? The Academic Spring and Scholarly Publishing in the Humanities and Social Sciences," *Publishing Research Quarterly* 28, 3 (September 2012): 159–171. Carolyn E. Lipscombe, "Mergers in the Publishing Industry," *Bulletin of the Medical Library Association* 89, 3 (July 2001): 307–308. David Matthews, "Is It Time to Nationalize Academic Publishers?," *The Times Higher Education*, March 2, 2018, https://www.timeshighereducation.com/blog/it-time-nationalise-academic-publishers.

21. Albert N. Greco and Alana M. Spendley, "The Price of University Press Books 2012–2014," *Journal of Scholarly Publishing* 47, 2 (January 2016): 106–120. Also see Ann Steiner, "The Global Book: Micropublishing, Conglomerate Production, and Digital Market Structures," *Publishing Research Quarterly* 34, 1 (March 2018): 118–132.
22. Michael Artiles, Christian Beaulieu, Samantha Carey, Madeline Danza, Andrew Gatian, Alexa Gavin, Albert N. Greco, Alexandra Jameson, Adam McWilliams, Kristen Samuelson, and Robert Wharton, "The Impact of E-Books and E-Readers on the Library of Congress and the U.S. Copyright Office," *Journal of Scholarly Publishing* 45, 1 (October 2013): 1–34.
23. Albert N. Greco, *Essential JSP: Critical Insights Into the World of Scholarly Publishing:* Vol. 3, *Scholarly Journals: Print, Digital, Open Access, and Search Engines* (Toronto: University of Toronto Press, 2012), 1–29. Also see Kathleen Shearer, "Responding to Unsustainable Journal Costs: A CARL Brief," CARL ABRC, 1–8, http://www.carl-abrc.ca/wp-content/uploads/2018/02/CARL_Brief_Subscription_Costs_en.pdf.
24. MacKensie Smith and Ivy Anderson, "Would an APC-Funded Business Model for Open Access Be Sustainable at Scale?," http://www.arl.org/storage/documents/mm16sp_Smith.pdf. Also see Karen M. Albert, "Open Access: Implications for Scholarly Publishing and Medical Libraries," *Bulletin of the Medical Library Association* 94, 3 (July 2006): 253–262. Matteo Migheli, "Open Access, Social Norms, and Publication Choice," *European Journal of Law and Economics* 35, 2 (April 2013): 149–167. Michael Hagner, "Open Access, Data Capitalism, and Academic Publishing," https://smw.ch/en/issue/edn/smw.2018.78. Claire DeMarco and Kyle Courtney, "Digital Publishing: A Home for Faculty in the Library—Exercises in Innovation from Harvard Law School," working paper, https://dash.harvard.edu?handle/1/34864118. Heather Piwowar, Jason Priem, Vincent Lariviere, Juan Pablo Alperin, Lisa Matthias, Bree Norlander, Ashley Farley, Jevin West, and Stephanie Haustein, "The State of OA: A Large-Scale Analysis of the Prevalence and Impact of Open Access Articles," PeerJ, 1–34, https://peerj.com/articles/4375.pdf,

doi:10.7717/peerj.4375. Patrick McCartan, "Journals and the Production of Knowledge: A Publishing Perspective," *British Journal of Political Science* 40, 2 (April 2010): 237–248. Alex Holcombe and Bjorn Brembs, "Open Access in Germany: The Best Deal Is No Deal," *The Times Higher Education*, December 27, 2017, https://www.timeshighereducation.com/blog/open-access-Germany-best-deal-no-deal.

25. Bo-Christer Bjork, "Evolution of the Scholarly Mega-Journal 2006–2017," PeerJ 6 (2018): ed4357. http://www.doi.org/10.7717/peerj.4357. Also see "Hybrid Journals Vital for Extending Author Choice, Research Shows," https://www.publishers.org/uk/media-centre/news-releases/2018/hybrid-journals-vital-for-extending-author-choice-research-shows. Aaron Edlin, "Competition Policy for Journals: The Bundling of Academic Journals," *American Economic Review* 95, 2 (May 2005): 441–446.
26. Prachi Shukla and Naved Ahmad, "Impact of Institutional Repositories on Scholarly Practices of Scientists," University of Nebraska-Lincoln Digital Commons, 1–7, https://digitalcommons.unl.edu/libphilprac/1631.
27. Catherine Barr and Jane Williams, eds., *The Bowker Annual: Library and Book Trade Almanac,* 40th ed. (New Providence, NJ: R. R. Bowker, 1995), 528–529.
28. US Department of Commerce, Bureau of the Census, "Monthly and Annual Retail Sales," https://www.census.gov/retail/index.html.
29. Albert N. Greco, Jim Milliot, and Robert M. Wharton, *The Book Publishing Industry,* 3rd ed. (New York and London: Routledge, 2014), 32–87.
30. Dave Bogart, ed., *The Library and Book Trade Almanac,* 60th ed. (New Providence, NJ: Information Today, 2015), 476–477.
31. US Department of Commerce, Bureau of the Census, "Monthly and Annual Retail Sales," https://www.census.gov/retail/index.html.
32. US Department of Labor, Bureau of Labor Statistics, https://data.bls.gov/timeseries/CUUR0000SA0L1E?output_view=pct_12mths.
33. Peter J. Dougherty, "Why Books Matter for the Long Run," knowledge@wharton.upenn.edu/article/vitality-books-long-run.
34. Margot Harrison, "Weighing the Losses of University Press of New England," https://www.sevendaysvt.com/vermont/weighing-the-losses-of-university-pres-of-new-england/Content?oid=24281275. Also see Alex Green, "University Press of New England to Close," *Publishers Weekly*, https://www.publishersweekly.com/pw/by-topic/industry-news/publisher-news/article/76660-university-press-of-new-england-to-close.html. Britta Green, "After Nearly 50 years, University Press of New England to Wind Down," https://www.nhpr.org/post/after-nearly-50-years-university-press-new-england-wind-down#stream/0.

35. Tina E. Chrzastowski, "The Serials Cancellation Crisis: National Trends in Academic Library Serial Collections," *Library Acquisitions: Practice & Theory* 21, 4 (1997): 431–443. Also see Brian W. Keith, "Statistical Analysis of Library Budgets," http://ufdc.ufl.edu/AA00019455.
36. Clifford A. Lynch, "Institutional Repositories: Essential Infrastructure for Scholarship in the Digital Age," *Portal: Libraries and the Academy* 3, 2 (2003): 327–336. Also see Jain Priti, "New Trends and Future Applications/Directions of Institutional Repositories in Academic Institutions," *Library Review* 60, 2 (2011): 125–141. Liat Klain Gabbay and Snunith Shoham, "The Role of Academic Libraries in Research and Teaching," *Journal of Librarianship and Information Science,* December 4, 2017, http://journal.sagepub.com/doi/abs/10.1177/0961000617742462.
37. Albert N. Greco, Amy Brand, and Robert M. Wharton, "Demographics of Scholarly Publishing and Communication Professionals," *Learned Publishing* 29, 2 (April 2016): 97–101.
38. Nicole Benevento, Albert N. Greco, Toniann Pasqueralle, Clara Rodriguez, Francesca Russo, Alana M. Spendley, Kelly Sullivan, Yiming Sun, and Robert M. Wharton, "Who Publishers More Books in U.S. English Departments, Men or Women?," *Publishing Research Quarterly* 33, 4 (December 2017): 357–372.
39. US Constitution, http://www.archives.gov/exhibits/charters/constitution_transcript.html.
40. US Const. Article 1 §8. Article 1 §8 forms the legal foundation for copyrights, patents, and trademarks. Also see William S. Strong, *The Copyright Book: A Practical Guide,* 6th ed. (Cambridge, MA: MIT Press, 2014), 1–46, 47–76, 227–272.
41. US Copyright Act of 1790, 1 Statutes at Large, 124; https://copyright.gov/about/1790-copyright-act.html. Also see Roger Schechter, *Intellectual Property: The Law of Copyrights, Patents, and Trademarks* (St. Paul, MN: West Academic Publishing, 2008), 5–81; Sheldon W. Halpern, *Copyright Law: Protection of Original Expression* (Durham, NC: Carolina Academic Press, 2010), 10–71; Amory, "The New England Book Trade," in *A History of the Book in America,* Vol. 1: *The Colonial Book in the Atlantic World,* 326.
42. US Copyright Office, Circular 1a: "United States Copyright Office: A Brief Introduction and History;" http://www.copyright.goc/circs/circ1a.html.
43. Ibid.
44. Ibid.
45. A complete copy of 17 U.S.C. is available at https://www.copyright.gov/title17, and it contains the text of Title 17 of the United States Code including all amendments enacted by Congress through December

2016. The US copyright law is contained in chapters 1 through 8 and 10 through 12 of Title 17 of the United States Code (17 U.S.C.).

46. Title 17 of the United States Code. Also see the Berne Convention for the Protection of Literary and Artistic Works. Article, http://www.wipo.int/treaties/en/ip/berne/summary/berne.html. Also see Albert N. Greco, *The Economics of the Publishing and Information Industries* (New York: Routledge, 2015), 259–287.
47. This law has been called the "Mickey Mouse Protection Act" since it extended the copyright protection for the cartoon character Mickey Mouse. See Lawrence Lessing, "Copyright's First Amendment," *UCLA Law Review* 48 (2001): 1057–1065.
48. Pub. L. 94–533; 17 U.S.C §§ 101–810, http://legislink.org/us/pl+94-553; 17 U.S.C §§ 101–81. Also see Cornell University Law School, "Copyright: Overview," https://www.law.cornell.edu/wex/copyright; Cornell University Law School, "Direct Infringement," https://www.law.cornell.edu/wex/direct_infringement; Cornell University Law School, "Secondary Liability," https://www.cornell.edu/wex/secondary_liability; Cornell University Law School, "Contributory Infringement," https://www.cornell.edu/wex/contributory_infringement; Intellectual Trademark Association, "Combating Contributory Infringement on the Internet," *INTA Bulletin* 69, 9 (May 1, 2014): 1–5; and US Copyright Office, http://www.copyright.gov; for circulars, http://www.copyright.gov/circs.
49. Pub. L., 105–298; 122 Stat.2827; 17 U.S.C. §§108 203(a), 301(c), 302, 303, 304(c)(2),: htttp://legislink.org/us/pl-105-298. Also see "Frequently Asked Questions About Copyright," https://www.copyright.gov/help/faq/index.html.
50. National Bureau of Economic Research, US Business Cycle Expansions and Contractions, http://www.nber.org/cycles.html.
51. Albert N. Greco and Chelsea Aiss, "University Presses in the 21st Century: The Potential Impact of Big Data and Predictive Analytics on Scholarly Book Marketing," *Journal of Scholarly Publishing* 46, 2 (January 2015): 105–140. Also see Victor Mayer-Schonberger and Thomas Ramge, "Are the Most Innovative Companies Just the Ones With the Most Data?," *Harvard Business Review Blog*, February 7, 2018, https://hbr.org/2018/02/are-the-most-innovative-companies-just=the-ones-with-the-most-data.

[2]

THE PRODUCT AND PRICING OF SCHOLARLY JOURNALS

INTRODUCTION: THE DEVELOPMENT AND GROWTH OF SCHOLARLY JOURNALS

In the last 350-plus years, as various fields of academic research developed and grew, the need for high-quality scholarly journals emerged to transmit the latest scientific discoveries and theories. This allowed scholarly journals to gain the preeminent foothold in scientific academic and research centers.

Ironically, the birth of the modern scholarly journal had a rather unusual and unplanned history. Around 1450, Johannes Gutenberg, in Mainz, Germany, developed the first efficient printing press utilizing a letterpress technology, specifically movable metal type, rather than wooden type faces.[1] This innovation allowed Gutenberg, and other printers in Europe, to print rather long print runs (at least by the standards of that era) because the type was composed of a relatively durable alloy of lead, tin, and antimony.[2] The second major innovation was the production and availability of reliable printing inks, and the third was durable paper able to withstand the pressure of a letterpress. Without Gutenberg's press (which was based on the wine press), printing inks, and printing paper, the scholarly journal would not have emerged in France and England in 1665.[3]

In January 1665, Jean-Denis de Sallo created the first scholarly science journal, *Journal des Savants*, publishing important articles in physics, chemistry, and the musing of scientists and philosophers. Fortunately, for scholars in the history of science and journal publishing, readable copies of the original 1665 issue up to 2010 are available on several French websites.[4]

Not to be outdone by their colleagues in France, the English Royal Society launched in March 1665 its *Philosophical Transactions of the Royal Society*.[5] The original purpose of this journal was similar to *Journal des Savants* in that it sought to provide a usable journal that published research studies and theories in the physical sciences and mathematics.[6] However, as scientific fields expanded, the Royal Society eventually reconfigured the *Philosophical Transactions of the Royal Society*, and the journal was expanded into two rather different publications. *Philosophical Transactions A* emphasized research papers in the physical sciences, mathematics, and engineering, whereas *Philosophical Transactions B* focused on the life sciences. Both journals are still published today, and both are highly ranked and considered two of the most important science journals in the world; the entire archive, back to the first issue in 1665, is available online.[7]

During the centuries following the creation of *Journal des Savants* and the *Philosophical Transactions of the Royal Society*, the number of scholarly journals grew at a rather slow pace. Donald W. King, Dennis D. McDonald, and Nancy K. Roderer estimated that the total number of journals in the world in 1830 was in the low hundreds, reaching only about 500 by the end of World War I, and about 1,000 by 1929.[8] For example, in the years 1939–1941, King, McDonald, and Roderer reported that academics in 1939 had access to about 1,500 scholarly journals.[9]

Albert Henderson wrote that, before September 1, 1939, Europe and not the United States was the global center of scientific, technical, and medical (known as STM) scholarly research, including such luminaries as Werner Heisenberg and Niels Bohr in physics; Otto Hahn in chemistry, radioactivity, and radiochemistry; Henri Bergson and Jacques Maritain in philosophy; and John Maynard Keynes in economics. In 1941, America was still dependent on European-based fundamental scientific research for much of its technological development. For example, German research laboratories and universities had impressive and advanced levels of inquiry in several major STM fields, notably chemistry and physics, producing high-impact research papers and attracting the best students from abroad.[10] Prior to America's entry into World War II, scholarly publications amounted to "luxury goods" available only in research libraries, to individuals who were members of an academic society, or to academics who shared access to a scholarly journal.[11]

In the 1939–1940 academic year, there were only 1,344 four-year colleges with an instructional staff of 110,885. Total college library expenditures were $19.5 million; total instructional and department research expenses were $280.2 million; and the book value of endowments for all US colleges was $1.77 billion.[12] The National Bureau of Economic Research (NBER) issued statistics that, in 1940, there were 1.25 million college students; 8.1 million Americans were unemployed; and the unemployment rate was 14.6%. The US Department of Commerce's Bureau of Economic Analysis (BEA) reported that, in 1940, the gross domestic product (GDP) stood at $11.2 billion in current, not chained, dollars; it was $14.9 billion in 1929.[13]

The United States has a long tradition in scholarly research and publications (e.g., Benjamin Franklin, Samuel F. B. Morse, Thomas A. Edison, etc.), and academic societies with publications programs (e.g., the *American Journal of Mathematics*, founded in 1878). Henderson pointed out that, in the 19th century, most journals in the United States were edited and published by academic societies, including the *American Anthropologist* (1888), the *Journal of Geology* (1893), and the *Astrophysical Journal* (1895).[14]

However, September 1945 represents the tipping point in the emergence of the United States as an important research market for and publisher of scholarly journals. Major scientific discoveries in the 20th century triggered the development of new journals in the scientific, technical, and medical fields as well as in two other major research categories, which included legal, tax, and regulatory journals (known as LTR) and in the humanities and the social sciences (known as HSS).

Today, there is an abundance of journals and scholarly platforms available to academics and researchers eager to publish their papers. This includes:

- 28,100-plus peer-reviewed print and digital English-language journals;[15]
- 6,450-plus peer-reviewed journals in other languages, and 2,500-plus are hybrid journals (allowing the author to pay an article publication/processing charge [APC] between $250 and $6,800 to retain the copyright and allow the article to be available freely to anyone in the world);[16]
- 1 million-plus scholarly article preprints (digital; e.g., http://www.arXiv.com, http://www.ssrn.com, http://ams.org/mathscinet, etc.);[17]
- 10,000-plus gold open access (OA) journals (all with APCs); certain publishers including Wolters Kluwer, Oxford University Press, and John Wiley offer OA gold journals, and they account for almost 14% of all OA journals;[18] and
- extensive academic library institutional repositories (digital; e.g., University of Michigan Library, Purdue University Library, etc.).

The National Science Foundation (NSF) estimated that about 2.2 million peer-reviewed scholarly articles were published in the world in 2013.[19] The World Bank provided some historical data on total science and technology journal output, which they estimated grew from slightly more than 974,000 in 2000 to 2.18 million in 2013 (slightly lower totals than the NSF estimates). This meant that, in 2013, 6,027 new articles were published every day, 251.14 every hour of the day, 4.19 every second, and an increase between

2000 and 2013 of 124.19%. Table 2.1 provides the data about journal output from the World Bank.[20] Mark Ware and Michael Mabe reported that academics in the United States in 2013 dominated total article output with a 23% share (about 506,000 articles); China was

Table 2.1 TOTAL GLOBAL OUTPUT OF SCHOLARLY JOURNAL ARTICLES, 2000–2013, AND ANNUAL PERCENT CHANGE

Year	Total Global Output of Scholarly Journals	Annual Percent Change
2000	974,348	—
2001	1,000,938	2.73%
2002	1,043,085	4.21%
2003	1,093,963	4.88%
2004	1,245,379	13.84%
2005	1,421,145	14.11%
2006	1,516,346	6.70%
2007	1,606,232	5.93%
2008	1,701,106	5.91%
2009	1,814,752	6.68%
2010	1,906,379	5.05%
2011	2,043,980	7.22%
2012	2,125,608	3.99%
2013	2,184,419	2.77%
2000–2013		124.19%

Source: The World Bank.

second with 17% (374,000); the United Kingdom was third with 7% (154,000).[21]

How did the scholarly journal sector grow from a modest number of journals (2 in Europe in 1665) into today's gigantic, global publishing community (of 44,500-plus journals and 1 million-plus preprint articles)?

THE BUSINESS OF SCHOLARLY JOURNAL PUBLISHING

This tremendous growth in scholarly journal publishing was the result of a series of unrelated and, ironically, unplanned events that started after the end of World War I, including the following:

1. There were significant developments in biology, chemistry, physics, and engineering in Germany, France, Italy, and the United Kingdom.
2. There was an increase in the number of major pieces of legislation, regulations, and agencies (e.g., the Communications Act of 1934 and the Federal Communications Commission [FCC]) in the United States in the years after the start of the Great Depression in October 1929.[22]
3. World War II had an impact on scientific, technical, and medical developments, which were incredibly significant, especially the development of STM nuclear research related directly to the atomic bomb and advances in medicine (e.g., the treatment of wounded members of the armed services and the physical rehabilitation of wounded veterans), important developments in economics because of the important work of John Maynard Keynes and Harry Dexter White at the Bretton Woods Conference in 1944, and the psychological and sociological work with military personnel during and after World War II.[23]
4. On June 22, 1944, President Roosevelt signed the Servicemen's Readjustment Act (frequently called the GI Bill of Rights). This

legislation provided returning men and women from the war a variety of education and technical training options, including college or professional school tuition, books, fees, and counseling services. The bill was created to strengthen educational opportunities in the United States and to prevent a recession or a depression when 16 million-plus members of the armed services returned to the United States. Ultimately, the GI Bill provided educational support for 2.3 million-plus Americans to attend college or graduate school. The GI Bill's impact on higher education was significant. Existing colleges offered new academic programs, some created branch campuses, and new colleges opened their doors, triggering the need for more faculty members and the creation of new or expanded existing college libraries. The number of academic degrees doubled between 1940 and 1950.[24]

5. There was an increase in the global number of academics and researchers.
6. As US colleges and universities experienced a period of rapid growth after 1945, a large number of institutions instituted a more rigorous process for tenure and promotion, specifically the acceptance of "publish or perish" procedures. This meant that, in the years after the end of World War II, one required journal article for tenure in certain areas of STM, LTR, and HSS morphed into a larger number, reaching 10 at many major research universities; the scholarly journal threshold for promotion to associate professor or full professor was higher.
7. The US government launched a number of major agencies and research centers to support scientific projects (e.g., the Atomic Energy Commission in 1946).[25]
8. Research institutes required researchers to apply for grants from the US government or foundations to support important projects, and the required number of grants and published scholarly journal articles increased to maintain employment at these facilities.

9. Academic societies and university presses responded to these developments by increasing the page count and number of issues for many of their journals; some created new journals to provide an outlet for academics and researchers working in developing academic fields.
10. The commercial academic publishers also expanded the number and scope of their journal operations to provide publishing platforms for the increased number of articles being produced in the United States and in the rest of the world.

THE QUEST FOR SCALE

Because of the growth in the number of faculty members and researchers producing more scholarly articles and journals, academic societies, university presses, and commercial scholarly publishers confronted the problem of scale. How could they increase the page count and the number of issues of an existing journal and/or launch a new journal or a series of journals in a specific academic category? Journal publishers knew that they needed to address the long-run average total cost curve by increasing output.[26] If this could be achieved, known as economies of scale to economists, distinct cost advantages could be created because fixed costs related to unit manufacturing costs could be spread over a larger number of journals. This would mean greater internal operational efficiencies and synergies since a journal office could handle editorial, art, design, layout, and production; the purchasing of printing, paper, and binding (PPB); and the costly warehousing and distribution for many different journals. In addition, the cost of capital could be reduced, which could allow for expansion and possibly the acquisition of other scholarly journals. Theoretically, there is a limit to the number of journals a publisher could handle efficiently, which is called "diseconomies of scale."[27]

It did not take long for faculty members and scientific researchers to realize that their future rested on producing a steady flow of journal articles, hopefully in high-impact journals. However, where should they submit an article? Eventually a publishing strategic framework emerged for eager academics and researchers interested in a publication:

1. Determining the prestige of a journal, its citation index, its editorial board, the number of "star" academics or researchers (e.g., Nobel Prize winners, academics at top-tier universities) who published in the journal, and its "reach" (i.e., the influence a journal has to get attention for the author within a specific academic community, or attention in the media, perhaps newspapers, magazines, or television)
2. Evaluating the probability of acceptance (did the article "fit" into the journal's academic niche and its target readership?)
3. Ascertaining the journal's turnaround from submission until peer review and publication (very important to a faculty member up for tenure or promotion)
4. Accepting a journal's submission fees or page fees for color reproduction of charts or photographs (submission fees are not commonly found with humanities journals and some LTR journals) and the journal language requirements (e.g., English?)
5. Understanding the impact if the journal was a "pay wall journal" (i.e., a journal that required a paid subscription fee to access the content) or was a gold OA journal (i.e., a journal that required the author to pay an APC, thereby allowing free access to the journal's content)
6. Pondering "other" considerations (e.g., if the journal were published by a company under a boycott by academics)

Of course, some academics and researchers in certain fields, especially astrophysics, high-energy physics, mathematical physics, nonlinear sciences, and quantum physics, appeared to prefer sending an early draft of an article to a preprint archive (e.g., http://www.arXiv.

org) because of the fast turnaround time of preprints. Other academic disciplines launched versions of arXiv, including sociology and law. In many instances, the preprint article would be submitted at a later time to a traditional journal. Some academics and researchers that received grants from the US government, a foreign government, or a funding organization could be obligated to submit the article to a gold OA journal, which explains the dramatic growth of PloS: "PloS was founded in 2001 as a nonprofit Open Access publisher, innovator and advocacy organization with a mission to accelerate progress in science and medicine by leading a transformation in research communication."[28]

MONEY NEVER SLEEPS

However, two problems had to be confronted by journal publishers. How could they create an impregnable "economic moat" to protect their journals against the constant threats posed by journal hackers and thieves? Where would they get the money to support increased output?

The importance of "economic moats" was discussed in some detail by Warren Buffett in a talk at the University of Florida in 2007. "I like businesses I can understand. . . . It doesn't make sense to go with things you think you can['t] understand. . . . I don't want a business that's easy for competitors. I want a business with a moat around it. I want a very valuable castle in the middle. . . . And then I want a big moat around the castle, and that moat can be various things."[29]

Again, scholarly journals benefited directly from yet another series of unrelated developments. First, in the years after the end of World War II, a number of nations experienced periods of economic stability and growth, for example, an increase in the GDP, relatively low unemployment rates, and increases in both exports and imports. And the total amount of money in the world increased, albeit rather slowly for several decades. While the total amount of money in the world is not known precisely, the best estimates are based on data released by the Bank for International Settlement (BIS). BIS monitors many datasets, including locational and consolidated banking statistics, derivatives statistics, global liquidity indicators, credit to the nonfinancial sector, debt service ratios for the private nonfinancial sector, property price statistics, and consumer prices. BIS estimated that there is between $70 trillion and $80 trillion in the world, although some estimates place the total at about $90 trillion.[30]

For example, in September 2018, Blackrock, the largest global asset manager, handled about $6.35 trillion-plus in assets under management (AUM) across different product lines and regions.[31] Sovereign wealth funds (SWFs) are state-owned investment funds. These funds vary in size. The five largest SWFs, according to the Sovereign Wealth Fund Institute, in late 2018 were the Norway Government Pension Fund, with $1,058 billion; the China Investment Corporation, with $941 billion; the Abu Dhabi Investment Authority, with $683 billion; the Kuwait Investment Authority, with $592 billion; and the Hong Kong Monetary Authority, with $523 billion. Total SWFs topped $7.4 trillion in September 2018.[32]

Second, money never sleeps, and asset fund managers must seek viable investments to develop high yields to generate an expected annual return on invested capital (ROIC). The growth in the scholarly journals sector, with rather interesting gross margins, caught the attention of fund managers, and many of them invested in several of the largest commercial scholarly publishing companies, allowing these journal operations to grow and take advantage of economies of scale.

The following is a partial list of investors for three major public commercial scholarly publishing firms; data was available as of December 2018:

1. RELX (formerly known as Reed Elsevier): Bank of America, Bank of New York Mellon Corporation, Lazard Asset Management, Northern Trust, Parametric Portfolio

Associates, Raymond James & Associates, and Wells Fargo & Co. Wolters Kluwer: Glenmede Trust Co. NA, Lazard Retirement Global Dynamic Multi-Asset Portfolio, Parametric Portfolio Associates, and Sextant International Fund
2. John Wiley & Sons: Blackrock, Franklin Resources, Fuller & Thaler Asset Management, State Street Corp., and Vanguard Group
3. Informa PLC: Fidelity Series International Growth Fund, Invesco International Growth Fund, Lazard International Strategic Equity Port, and Vanguard International Stock Index-Total Intl. Stock Index[33]

Academic societies and university presses had to develop their own sources of capital from internal or external sources, perhaps shifting revenues from book sales, conference revenues, distribution operations, government or private foundation grants, endowments, or gifts from alumni and individuals interested in the mission of the society or press.

SCHOLARLY PUBLISHERS DEVELOP A STRATEGY

Considering the managerial, marketing, and financial challenges scholarly publishers confronted, it was inevitable that many scholarly publishers had to develop long-term global strategies to address their concerns about scale and the structures needed to implement these strategies. Many of these publishers paid attention to several major authors who addressed some of these strategic concerns, including Alfred D. Chandler, Peter Drucker, and Michael E. Porter.

Alfred D. Chandler, winner of the Pulitzer Prize in 1978, studied the business and economic history of the United States, and he developed several major theories: (1) a firm's structure must follow the carefully developed strategy, and (2) the well-known "M-Form"—that is, a company creates and manages a series of relatively independent strategic business units (SBUs) that are charged with handling structural issues, including inbound logistics, operations, outbound logistics, marketing, services, procurement, technology issues, human resource management, and accounting, financial, legal, and government affairs.[34]

Peter Drucker eschewed the classic "command and control" procedures created by several major corporations (e.g., Harold Geneen in the 1960s and 1970s at IT&T) and macroeconomics. Instead, he stressed the role and function of the manager as a "knowledge worker," the need for meticulous planning before implementing a structure, that the purpose of a business was to satisfy the wants and needs of customers, and that a company should decide objectively what it does best and outsource any other function.[35]

Michael E. Porter's "Five Forces" outlined clearly and simply the substantive issues that a publisher needed to consider in creating a strategy and a structure, including (1) supplier power (e.g., authors submitting an article, printers, distributors, etc.), (2) barriers to entry into a market (e.g., legal issues in a specific market), (3) the threat of substitutes (i.e., another publisher publishing a journal in the same niche at a lower price), (4) buyer power (the ability of a library to cancel a journal's subscription), and (5) the degree of rivalry (the level of competition in a sector).[36]

Clearly, the ideas of Chandler, Drucker, and Porter influenced myriad managers to consider strategic issues related to the "marketing mix," known as the "4 Ps" (i.e., product, price, placement, and promotion), as well as the following:

1. Product differentiation: The publisher had to create a journal with a unique value proposition (i.e., create a journal that was superior to any competing journal to differentiate it in the marketplace) and needed a well-established scholar to be the editor-in-chief as well as associate and assistant editors with national and/or international reputations.

2. Pricing strategy: The publisher needed to create a pricing objective; determine demand for the journal; estimate production costs, both fixed and variable, and the breakeven point; analyze competitors' costs, prices, and competing journals in the same sector; select a realistic pricing method; and select the final price, which can vary from one subscriber to another (called "price discrimination" by economists). Options include "value pricing" (a low price), the "going-rate price" (charged by competitors), or a "premium price" (based on the perception of readers and librarians about the high quality of the journal).
3. Placement: The publisher had to craft a domestic and global distribution program (logistics).
4. Promotion: The publisher needed a well-established advertising and marketing strategy to make sure potential readers and librarians were aware of the journal. This meant direct-mail pieces, social media placements, advertisements in conference programs, booths at conferences, and so forth.

Wolters Kluwer is an example of a major commercial scholarly publisher that adopted many of these ideas to develop an effective global strategy. The essential key points of their strategic priorities for 2016–2018 include the following:

1. "expand market coverage: allocate capital to leading growth units and digital products; extend into adjacencies and new geographies; broaden sales and marketing coverage; and supplement organic growth with portfolio actions;
2. deliver expert solutions: deliver solutions providing improved outcomes and productivity; accelerate development of global and cloud solutions; expand new media marketing channels; and invest 8%–10% of revenues in innovation; and
3. drive efficiencies and engagement: drive scale economies, quality and agility; leverage our technology investments; and foster employee engagement."[37]

All of the major commercial scholarly publishers, as well as many societies and university presses, developed a wide variety of strategies. The commercial publishers stressed the acquisition of small journals and/or small to medium-sized competitors. Some prominent examples of publishers' active acquisitions include Academic Press, Cell Press, Gordon & Breach, Marcel Decker, Lippincott Williams & Wilkins, Nature Publishing, Springer, Blackwell, and Taylor & Francis.[38] Once a publisher had a cluster of important journals and scale, various pricing strategies were tested and, if successful, implemented. One example includes a prominent Elsevier STM journal *Brain Research,* which has an impact factor of 3.125. Its institutional subscription (as of March 2019) was $12,128, and this subscription fee excludes any discount or the average fee in a bundle of journals (known as the "big deal").[39]

While individual prices are useful, the average cost for journals in a specific category illustrates the pricing strategies of all publishers active in an academic field. The following figures contain data on the annual average costs for a library to subscribe to a very large number of philosophy journals.[40] The years used were the academic year; therefore, 2003 refers to the 2002–2003 academic year. The first cluster of journals was in the humanities, which generally have lower annual subscription prices than journals in the social sciences or the STM fields. In Figure 2.1, in 2003 the average subscription for philosophy journals hovered at the $150 mark, reaching almost $450 in 2016. Figure 2.2 addressed history journals, which had a very similar price structure as philosophy, and prices for both philosophy and history jumped about 193% between 2003 and 2016. However, Figure 2.3 includes journals in the language and literature field, and they had a different pricing pattern than the first two humanities journals. In 2003, it cost about $140, increasing to slightly more than about $370 in 2016 (+168%, lagging behind philosophy and history). Clearly, a publisher evaluates the potential number of libraries that could subscribe; the potential number of readers, academics and students, of a journal; and how a specific journal is valued. Society journals generally have a lower subscription fee than nonsociety journals, and

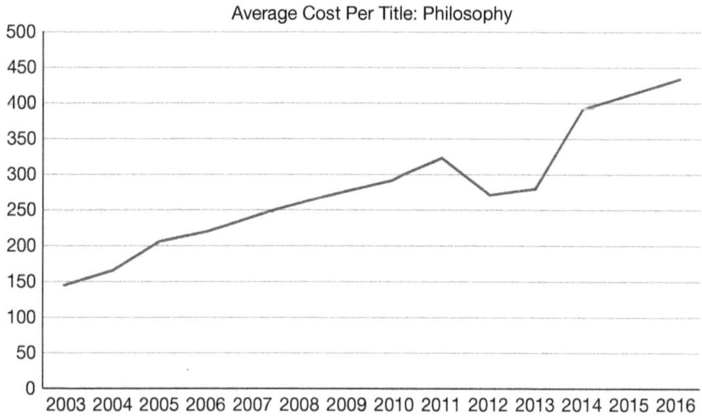

Figure 2.1 Average cost of philosophy journals, 2003–2016.

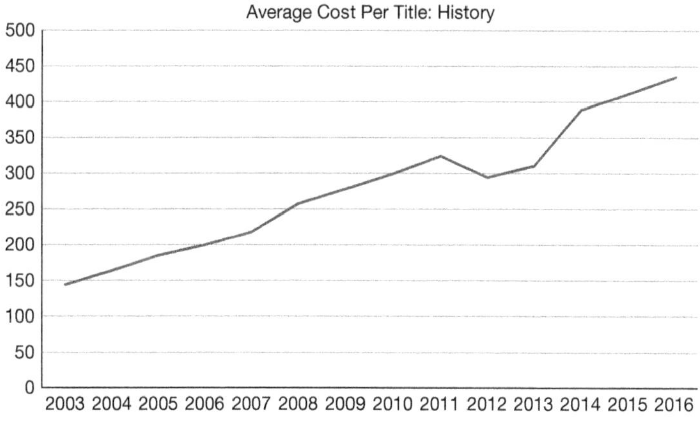

Figure 2.2 Average cost of history journals, 2003–2016.

membership in a society often includes a subscription to a journal published by the society.

The next group of journals were in the social sciences. Psychology's 2003 pricing data in Figure 2.4 of $400 was far more aggressive than those in the humanities, exceeding the $1,000 mark by 2016, representative of the fact that psychology is often considered a scientific

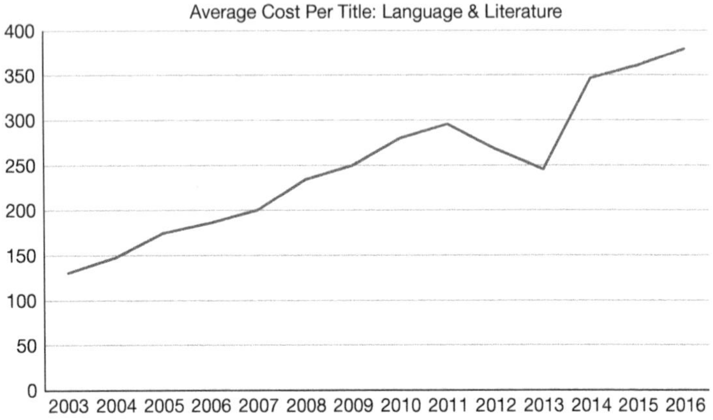

Figure 2.3 Average cost of language and literature journals, 2003–2016.

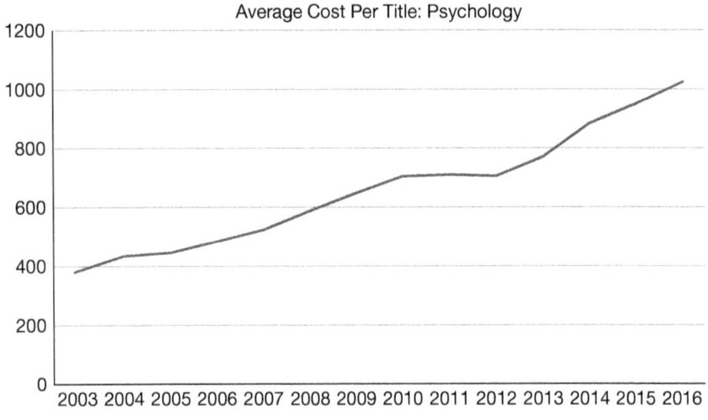

Figure 2.4 Average cost of psychology journals, 2003–2016.

field, and costs associated with many psychology journals are high because of production costs associated with formulas and color photographs. Business and economics journals, as seen in Figure 2.5, is one of the largest academic fields, and these journals had prices that increased only about 142% (far more modest than the humanities) between 2003 (about $600) and 2016 (about $1,450). Sociology, on

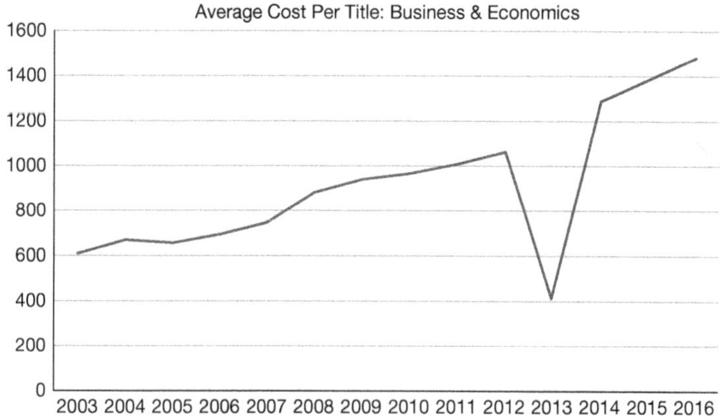

Figure 2.5 Average cost of business and economics journals, 2003–2016.

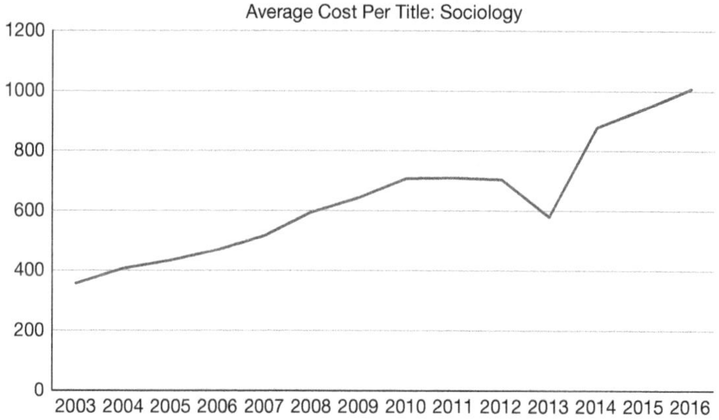

Figure 2.6 Average cost of sociology journals, 2003–2016.

the other hand, in Figure 2.6, lagged behind business and economics, reaching about $1,000 in 2016, up from about $400 in 2003 (+150%).

The last academic field includes two journal categories in the STM field. Mathematics and computer science in Figure 2.7 are academic disciplines that attract a large number of students in both the social sciences and STM. The results revealed the ability of publishers

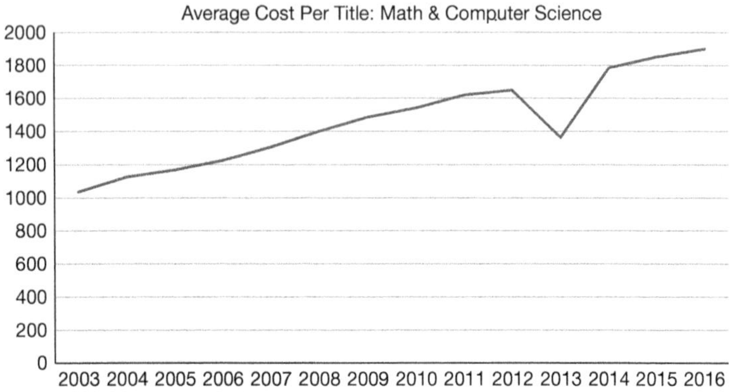

Figure 2.7 Average cost of mathematics and computer science journals, 2003–2016.

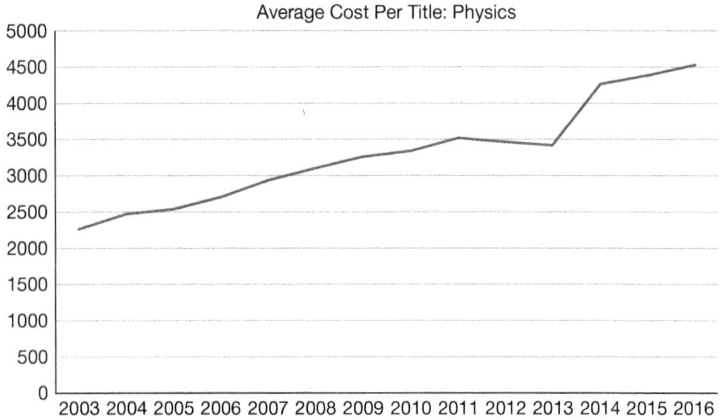

Figure 2.8 Average cost of physics journals, 2003–2016.

to charge large subscription prices, partially due to costs associated with setting type for complex mathematical formulas, and the frequency of publishing certain major journals in this cluster. In 2003, these journals cost slightly more than $1,000, reaching about $1,900 (+90%) in 2006. Physics, in Figure 2.8, commanded premium subscription prices, ranging from about $2,200 in 2003 to about $4,500 in 2016 (+105%), because of the frequency of the journals, to get relevant papers released in a timely manner, and expensive costs associated with complex mathematical formulas and color photographs/slides.

THE RESULTS

In the 1980s, scholarly journal publishing became a business, and an exceptionally big business. Lutz Bornmann and Ruediger Mutz analyzed historical scholarly journal output trends, and they posited that annual scholarly journal output stood at 1% in the middle of the 18th century, reached 2% to 3% between 1914 and 1945, and posted a torrid pace of 8% to 9% between 1945 and 2012.[41] Mark Ware and Michael Mabe estimated that global STM revenues reached about $10 billion in 2013, and about 55% of total STM revenues were from the United States (about $5.50 billion), 28% from Europe/the Middle East ($2.8 billion), 14% from Asia/Pacific ($1.4 billion), and 4% from the rest of the world ($400 million). In 2013, the United States accounted for LTR revenues of about $2.03 billion and HSS revenues of about $920 million. Ware and Mabe also estimated that there were between 5,000 and 10,000 STM "publishers globally, of which around 5,000 are included in the important Scopus database; Elsevier's Scopus is the largest abstract and citation database of peer-reviewed literature. The main English-language trade and professional associations for journal publishers collectively include about 650 publishers."[42]

Outsell (a publishing research organization) also developed revenue estimates; their results differed somewhat from Ware and Mabe. Outsell estimated that in 2013, total global STM revenues (which include scientific and technical journals, geophysical journals, and medical journals in English and in other languages) topped $32.5 billion, and in 2014 revenues grew 3.6%, reaching $33.7 billion. Outsell's projections for the years 2015 through 2018 are impressive:

2015, \$35.05 billion (+4.01%); 2016, \$36.56 billion (+4.31%); 2017, \$38.13 billion (+4.29%); and 2018, \$39.84 billion (+4.48%).[43] In 2014, the United States accounted for 42.8% (\$14.4 billion) of total STM revenues, with the rest of the Americas reaching \$2.1 billion (6.1%). Europe's totals stood at \$11.5 billion (34%), and Asia and the Pacific Rim reached 17.1% (\$5.6 billion).[44] Overall, journal revenues were generated primarily by library subscriptions (between 68% and 75% of total revenues), corporate subscriptions (15% to 17%), advertising (4%), personal subscriptions (3%), and article processing changes (APCs; 3%).[45]

PAYWALL AND GOLD OPEN ACCESS JOURNALS

With traditional paid subscription journals with a paywall, the author conveys the copyright to the publisher, and the publisher covers all expenses associated with the publication of the article. In the United States, the copyright law (17 U.S.C.) stipulates that the publisher owns the copyright for the life of the author and 70 years after the author dies.[46] The procedure is different with "gold" OA journals; the author retains the copyright and is charged an APC. The article is available for free to a reader/library. Funds for APCs are from research grants, university or research organizations, funding bodies, schools/colleges, or academic departments, or are directly paid by the researcher(s). APCs vary significantly. Some APC examples in December 2018 include the following:

1. John Wiley journals: *Advanced Science*: \$5,000; *Cancer Medicine*: \$2,500; *Journal of Medical Radiation Sciences*: \$1,900; *Molecular Oncology*: \$3,000; *Thoracic Cancer*: \$2,200[47]
2. PloS journals: *PloS Biology*: \$2,900; *PloS Medicine*: \$2,900; *PloS Computational Biology*: \$2,250; *PloS Genetics*: \$2,250; *PloS Pathogens*: \$2,250; *PloS Neglected Tropical Diseases*: \$2,250; *PloS One* \$1,495[48]

Hybrid journals are a traditional journal with a paywall, but this journal offers the author the gold OA option for an APC, and the author retains the copyright if the APC is paid. In February 2013, the Holdren Memo was issued directing all US government departments and agencies (with research budgets of $100 million-plus annually) to make all nonsecret US government–funded research available for free to the public for one year after the research was published in a scholarly journal. The European Union also mandated OA research publication guidelines.[49]

Some journals require a submission fee to cover the costs associated with the review and publication processes. Many major research universities provide financial support (i.e., a subvention) for faculty members to cover journal submission fees (generally between $250 and $500-plus) and/or page charges (a fee for every letter or character in an article) and/or color figure charges. Some examples of major economics journals with submission fees, as of December 2018, include *American Economic Review*: $190 for nonmembers and $100 for members; *Journal of Economic History*: $50 for nonmembers and no fee for members; and the *Rand Journal of Economics*: $100 for nonmembers and $85 for members.[50]

Many STM journals require "publication" fees that cover the costs associated with reproducing color figures. Table 2.2 lists these fees for various STM journals.

If an author wants to utilize the "gold" OA option and/or has to submit a journal submission fee but lacks the funds to cover the fee, many journals (e.g., Elsevier) will review individual waiver requests on a case-by-case basis. However, priority for this waiver program will be given to applications by authors from countries eligible for the Research4Life program.[51] The major commercial scholarly publishers, utilizing a variety of strategies and effective marketing, financial, and technological structural plans, grew significantly.[52] The following material in Tables 2.3–2.5 was released by four public corporations in a series of required financial statements, and all this information is available on their website.

Table 2.2 JOURNAL ARTICLE PAGE FEES: 2018 (US DOLLARS)

Journal	*Article Fees*
American Journal of Physiology	$85.00/page; $200.00 color figure
Cancer Research	$1,500.00; $675.00 color figure
Cell	$1,000.00 for first color figure
	$275.00 each added color figure
Cellular and Molecular Gastroenterology and Hepatology	$2,000.00; $1,200 for members
Journal of Biological Chemistry	$95.00/; $50.00 for each figure
Nature Cell Biology	$650.00 first color figure
	$310.00 each added color figure
PLOS Biology	$2,900.00 an article

Source: M. Bishr Omary and Theodore S. Lawrence, "Opinion: Understanding and Coping With Rising Publication Costs," https://www.the-scientist.com/critic-at-large/opinion-understanding-and-coping-with-rising-pubolication-costs-30238.

Table 2.3 outlines the financial status of RELX, formerly known as Reed Elsevier or Elsevier until 2015; however, the company is still called Elsevier within the publishing community. Elsevier is more than a scholarly journal publisher; it has the following business operating units: STM, risk and analytics, legal, exhibitions (trade shows including Book Expo America), and unallocated items. Between 2014 and 2017, RELX posted increases in total revenues, +27.4%; cost of revenue, +31.06%; gross profit, +25.4%; selling general and administrative, +18.83%; total operating profit, +24.42%; and operating income, 37.16%.

Table 2.3 RELX COMBINED BUSINESSES (£ MILLIONS, DECEMBER 31, 2017)

	2017	*2016*	*2015*	*2014*
Revenues	7,355	6,895	5,971	5,773
Cost of revenue	2,631	2,488	2,129	2,006
Gross profit	4,724	4,407	3,842	3,767
Selling general and administrative	2,871	2,750	2,430	2,416
Total operating expenses	5,502	5,238	4,559	4,422
Operating income or loss	1,853	1,657	1,412	1,351

N.B.: All numbers rounded off and may not always equal 100%.

Source: RELX Group Annual Reports and Financial Statements, https://www.relx.com/~/media/Files/R/RELX-Group/documents/reports/annual-reports/relx2017-annual-report.pdf; also see

https://www.relx.com/˜/media/Files/R/RELX-Group/documements/reports/annual-reports/relx2016-annual-report.pdf; https://www.relx.com/˜/media/Files/R/RELX-Group/documements/reports/annual-reports/2015-annual-report.pdf; https://www.relx.com/˜/media/Files/R/RELX-Group/documements/reports/annual-reports/2014-annual-report.pdf; https://www.relx.com/˜/media/Files/R/RELX-Group/documements/reports/annual-reports/2013-annual-report.pdf.

Informa PLC's financial information is shown in Table 2.4; Informa also has a number of SBUs in addition to its well-established journal unit. Informa posted strong results between 2014 and 2017: revenues, +54.53%; cost of revenue, +105.53%; gross profit,

Table 2.4 INFORMA PLC COMBINED BUSINESSES (£ IN MILLIONS, DECEMBER 31, 2017)

	2017	*2016*	*2015*	*2014*
Revenues	1,757	1,345	1,212	1,137
Cost of revenue	1,412	788	711	687
Gross profit	345	557	500	449
Selling general and administrative	N/A	25	20	19
Total operating expenses	1,412	1,046	944	896
Operating income or loss	345	299	267	140

N.B.: Estimates for 2016. All numbers rounded off and may not always equal 100%.

Source: Annual Reports and Financial Statements, https://informa.com/Documents/Investor%20Relations/2018/results/Informa%20PLC%202017%20Consolidated%20Financial%20Statements.pdf; also see https://informa.com/Documents/Investor%20Relations/2017/Informa%202016%20Full%20Year%20Results%20Statement.pdf; https://informa.com/Documents/Investor%20Relations/2017/Informa_Annual_Report_2016.pdf.

–23.16%; selling general and administrative, N/A; total operating profit, +57.59%; and operating income, +146.43%.

John Wiley's SBUs include various products including books and journals. Wiley's recorded cost of revenue for 2015 to 2018, shown in Table 2.5, was –1.43%; cost of revenue, –2.81%; gross profit, –0.91%; selling general and administrative, –1.39%; total operating profit, –2.06%; and operating income, +1.87%.

Table 2.5 JOHN WILEY & SONS, COMBINED BUSINESSES ($ MILLIONS, APRIL 30, 2018)

	2018	*2017*	*2016*	*2015*
Revenues	1,796	1,719	1,727	1,822
Cost of revenue	485	461	466	499
Gross profit	1,311	1,258	1,261	1,323
Selling general and administrative	991	984	994	1,005
Total operating expenses	1,524	1,494	1,510	1,556
Operating income or loss	272	224	217	267

N.B.: All numbers rounded off and may not always equal 100%.

Source: Annual Reports (10-K) and Financial Statements, http://www.annualreports.com/Company/john-wiley-sons-inc; also see http://www/wiley.com/legacy/about/corpnews/FY17_30.

A SCHOLARLY JOURNAL PROFIT AND LOSS STATEMENT

Table 2.6 outlines the revenues and expenses for a well-established printed US business and economics journal owned by a nonprofit academic society, which is known as a 501(c) 3 entity under Internal Revenue Service (IRS) guidelines. But the society had a contract with a global scholarly journal publisher to handle the noneditorial functions, that is, maintenance of a computer system to handle submissions, advertising and sales, subscription collection, the posting of articles on a secure website, and negotiations with content aggregators (e.g., Project Muse) to distribute the content via web servers, as well as printing, paper, binding, warehousing, and distribution costs for the printed journal.

This journal was originally published by the society, but the business-related tasks proved to be a burden to the staff, so the society put the journal out for bid. It is quite common for societies to put out for bid a journal since there is intense competition from university presses and commercial publishers to publish a high-impact prestigious journal and to maintain scale in publishers' operations.

While various university presses and commercial scholarly publishers were very interested and submitted competitive bids, the highest bid, with the best distribution ratios of any surplus, was from a university press. Under the terms of the contract, the society would receive 75% of any surplus, and the publisher's share was 25%. The contract was for a five-year period, with the publisher willing to negotiate another five-year contract if both parties were satisfied with the quality of services offered by the publisher, the surplus percentage proved to be very satisfactory to the society, and the publisher had an opportunity to make a profit.

As indicated in Table 2.6, between 2014 and 2018, the society earned a very steady annual revenue stream, with a total of $1,152,228. These revenues allowed the journal to help subsidize various activities of the society, including regional meetings, a national convention, and various organizational expenses (e.g., staff salaries, fringe benefits, etc.). The publisher covered some of its expenses as well as a very impressive share of the annual surplus (i.e., $384,077).

If this journal went 100% digital, which is possible at some point, there could be additional cost savings. Plant expenditures (i.e., editorial, art, design, and layout) would remain the same, with the society handling only editorial and the publisher in charge of the other three. The savings would be with costs related to the following: (1) postage, (2) digital distribution (while digital distribution would have costs, they would be significantly lower since the physical warehousing and

Table 2.6 PROFIT AND LOSS (P&L) STATEMENT FOR A US CONTRACT SCHOLARLY JOURNAL (IN US DOLLARS)

	2014	*2015*	*2016*	*2017*	*2018*
Revenues					
1. Advertising Sales	12,383	12,657	12,912	13,184	13,533
2. Subscriptions	580,785	612,728	646,165	681,926	719,704
3. All other income	9,276	9,659	10,065	10,486	10,923
(Net commissions)					
Total	602,444	635,044	699,142	705,596	744,160
Cost of goods sold (COGS)					
1. Plant	85,246	89,576	93,931	98,495	103,282
2. Postage and distribution	15,447	15,791	16,124	16,447	16,777
3. Reprints	2,586	2,637	2,690	2,744	2,797
4. Direct mail promotion	12,000	12,500	12,900	13,300	13,700
5. Honoraria and office support	60,733	61,957	63,273	64,639	66,027
6. General and administrative overhead	105,618	111,487	117,569	124,622	131,410
Total	281,630	293,948	306,487	320,247	333,993
Gross margin	46.75%	46.29%	43.84%	45.39%	44.88%

Continued

Table 2.6 CONTINUED

	2014	*2015*	*2016*	*2017*	*2018*
Surplus (Loss)					
1. Total	281,6300	293,948	306,487	320,247	333,993
2. Share of surplus to society (75%)	211,222	220,461	229,865	240,185	250,495
3. Share of surplus to contract publisher (25%)	70,408	73,487	76,622	80,062	83,498

N.B.: This is a prominent journal in the business and economics category. The editor provided this data. Data for 2018 estimated by the editor. All numbers rounded off and may not always equal 100%.

distribution expenditures associated with a print journal would disappear), and (3) potential reductions in various promotion activities if online operations had lower costs and/or better reach results.

NOTES

1. Elizabeth L. Eisenstein, *The Printing Press as an Agent of Change* (Volumes 1 and 2 in One) (Cambridge: Cambridge University Press, 1980), 22–182.
2. Elizabeth L. Eisenstein, *The Printing Revolution in Early Modern Europe* (Cambridge: Cambridge University Press, 2012), 78–115.
3. Jeremiah E. Dittmar, "Information Technology and Economic Change: The Impact of the Printing Press," *Quarterly Journal of Economics* 126 (2011): 1133–1172.
4. Copies of the *Journal des Savants* are available for the years 1665–1944; see http://gallica.bnf.fr/ark:12148/cb343488023/date; for the years 1909-2010 and http://www.persee.fr/collection/jds. For access to the

modern version of the *Journal des Savants,* see http://www.persee.fr/web/revues/home/presscript/revue/jds. Also see David Banks, "Approaching the *Journal des Savants*, 1665–1695: A Manual Analysis of Thematic Structure," *Journal of World Languages* 2, 1 (2015): 1–17; Jean-Pierre Vittu, *"Du Journal des Savants aux Memoires Pour L'Historie des Sciences et des Beaux-Arts: L'Esquisse d'un Systeme Europeen des Periodiques Savants," Dix-Septieme Siecle* 3 (2005): 527–545.

5. See the Royal Society's website for historical information: https://royalsociety.org/about-us/history. Its list of authors includes Isaac Newton (in 1672); Charles Darwin (1837); Michael Faraday (1857); James Clerk Maxwell (1865); Alan Turing (1952); and Stephen Hawking (1983).
6. Roger Philip McCutcheon, "The *Journal des Savants* and the *Philosophical Transactions of the Royal Society," Studies in Philology* 21, 4 (October 1924): 626.
7. For information about *Philosophical Transactions A* and *Philosophical Transactions B,* see http://rsta.royalsocietypublishing.org/about. Also see the Royal Society's website for information: https://collections.royalsociety.org/?dsqIni=Dserve.ini&dsqApp=Library&dsqDb=Catalog&dsqCmd=Overview.tcl&dsqSearch=(text)%3d%27first+issue%27); and the Royal Society: http://rstb.royalsocietypublishing.org/citation-metrics.
8. Donald W. King, Dennis D. McDonald, and Nancy K. Roderer, *Scientific Journals in the United States: Their Production, Use, and Economics* (Stroudsburg, PA: Hutchinson Ross Publishing Company, 1981), 165.
9. Ibid., 319. Also see King Research, *Journal in Scientific Communication: The Role of Authors, Publishers, Libraries, and the Reader in a Vital System* (Washington, DC: National Science Foundation, 1979), 7–21; and King Research, *Statistical Indicators of Scientific and Technical Communication: 1960–1980* (Washington, DC: National Science Foundation, 1976), 54–60; and David A. Kronick, "Scientific Journals: A Review Article," *Library Quarterly: Information, Communication, Policy* 52, 3 (July 1982): 265–269.
10. Albert Henderson, "Diversity and the Growth of Serious Scholarly Scientific Journals," in *Scholarly Publishing: Books, Journals, Publishers, and Libraries in the Twentieth Century*, ed. Richard E. Abel, Lyman W. Newlin, Katrina Strauch, and Bruce Strauch (New York: John Wiley & Sons, 2002), 134–148.
11. Albert Henderson, "The Growth of Printed Literature in the Twentieth Century," in *Scholarly Publishing: Books, Journals, Publishers, and Libraries in the Twentieth Century*, ed. Richard E. Abel, Lyman W. Newlin, Katrina Strauch, and Bruce Strauch (New York: John Wiley & Sons, 2002), 1–23.
12. US Department of Commerce, *The Statistical Abstract of the United States 1950* (Washington, DC: Bureau of the Census, 1950), 124–133.

13. Stanley Lebergott, "Annual Estimates of Unemployment in the United States 1900–1954," in *The Measurement and Behavior of Unemployment* (Cambridge, MA: National Bureau of Economic Research, 1857), 211–242, http://www.nber.org/chapters/c2644. Also see US Department of Commerce, *The Statistical Abstract of the United States 1950* (Washington, DC: Bureau of the Census, 1950), 183–219. Also see US Department of Commerce, *Survey of Current Business 1942* (Washington, DC: Bureau of Foreign and Domestic Commerce, 1942), 8–11; and US Department of Commerce, *Survey of Current Business August 2012* (Washington, DC: Bureau of Economic Analysis, 2012), 183–209.
14. Henderson, "The Growth of Printed Literature in the Twentieth Century," 19–23.
15. Mark Ware and Michael Mabe, *The STM Report: An Overview of Scientific and Scholarly Journal Publishing 2015* (The Hague, Netherlands: International Association of Scientific, Technical, and Medicals Publishers, 2015), 6, http;//www.stm-assoc-0rg/2015_02_20_STM_Report_2015_pdf.
16. Ibid. Also see Mark Ware and Michael Mabe, *The STM Report: An Overview of Scientific and Scholarly Journal Publishing* (The Hague, Netherlands: International Association of Scientific, Technical, and Medicals Publishers, 2012), 19; and Mark Ware, *Scientific Publishing in Transition: An Overview of Current Developments* (Bristol, UK: Mark Ware Consulting Ltd., 2006), 3–4.
17. For general information about arXiv, see https://arxiv.org/help/general.
18. Directory of Open Access Journals: see https://doaj.org.
19. National Science Foundation, *Science and Engineering Indicators 2014* (Washington, DC: National Science Board, 2014), https://www.nsf.fov/statistics/seind14/imndex.cfm/chapter-5/c5s4.htm; also see National Science Foundation, *Science and Engineering Indicators 2012* (Washington, DC: National Science Board, 2012), https://www.nsf.fov/statistics/seind12/pdf/overview.pdf; and Alexandra Witze, "Research Gets Increasingly International," *Nature*, January 19, 2016, http://www.nature.com/news/research-get-increasingly-international-1.19198.
20. World Bank, http://www/data/worldbank.org/indicaor/IP.JRN.ARTC.SC. Also see Bo-Christer Bjork, Annikki Roos, and Mari Kauri, "Scientific Journal Publishing: Yearly Volume and Open Access," *Information Research* 14, 1 (March 2009), http://www.informationr.net/ir/14-1/paper391.html; Li Zhang, "China Leading the World for Growth in High-Quality Science Output, Nature Index," *Nature* press release, http://www.nature.com/press_release/nature-index-china-2015.html; Richard Van Noordan, "Global Scientific Output Doubles Every Nine

Years," *Nature* news blog, http://blogs.nature.com/news/2014/05/global-scientific-output0doubles-every-nine-years.

21. Ware and Mabe, *The STM Report: An Overview of Scientific and Scholarly Journal Publishing 2015,* 6–7. For a complete list of scholarly journal output by country, see Nature, *The Nature Index 2016*, http://www.natureindex.com/annual-tables/2016/country/all; for a complete list of scholarly journals by 500 academic institutions, see http://www.natureindex.com/annual-tables/2016/institution/academic/all.
22. The Communication Act of 1934, https://transition.fcc.gov/Reports/1934new.pdf.
23. Roger Daniels, *Franklin D. Roosevelt: The War Years, 1939–1945* (Urbana: University of Illinois Press, 2016), 74, 451. Also see Arthur Herman, *Freedom's Forge: How American Business Produced Victory in World War II* (New York: Random House, 2013), 107–144; and Maury Klein, *A Call to Arms: Mobilizing America for World War II* (New York: Bloomsbury Press, 2013), 463–622.
24. "The Servicemen's Readjustment Act (1944)," https://www.ourdocuments.gov/doc.php?flash=false&doc=76.
25. United States Nuclear Regulatory Commission, the Atomic Energy Commission, https://www.nrc.gov/reading-rm/basic-ref/glossary/atomic-energy-commission.html.
26. Paul Krugman, "Scale Economies, Product Differentiation, and the Pattern of Trade," *American Economic Review* 70, 5 (December 1980): 950–959. Also see John C. Panzar and Robert D. Willig, "Economies of Scale in Multi-Output Production," *Quarterly Journal of Economics* 91, 3 (1977): 481–493; and Rana Salman Anwar and Salman Ali, "Economies of Scale," *International Interdisciplinary Journal of Scholarly Research* 1, 1 (2015): 51–58.
27. J. E. Meade, "External Economics and Diseconomies in a Competitive Situation," *Economic Journal* 62, 245 (March 1952): 54–67.
28. PloS One, journal information, http://journals.plos.org/plosone/s/journal-information. Also see "General Information About arXiv," https://arxiv.org/help/general; David M. Maslove, "Medical Preprints—A Debate Worth having," *Journal of the American Medical Association* 319, 5 (2018): 443–444; Bonnie Swoger, "Understanding Your Rights: Pre-Prints, Post-Prints; and Publisher Versions," https://blogs.scientificamerican.com/information-culture/understanding-your-rights-pre-prints-post-prints -and-publisher-versions; Sandra Hopps and Allison Leung, "The Role of Preprints in Academic Publishing," https://connection-sagepub.com/blog/sage-connection/2018/11/30/the-role-of-preprints-in-academic-publishing; Philip N. Cohen, "SocArXiv Launches, Brings Sociology and Social Sciences Into The

Open, With New Grant Support," https://socopen.org/2016//12/07/socarxiv-launches-brings-social-science-out-into-the-open.

29. David Foulke, "Warren Buffett on Economic Moats," *Alpha Architect,* http://www.valuewalk.com/2015/09/warren-buffett-on-economic-moats; also see Albert N. Greco, *The Economics of the Publishing and Information Industries* (New York: Routledge, 2015), 33–58.
30. Bank for International Settlement, "BIS Statistical Bulletin, June 2017," https://www.bis.org/statistics/bulletin1706.htm; also see Bank for International Settlements, "Highlights of the BIS International Statistics," *BIS Quarterly Review,* June 6, 2017, https://www.bis.org/publ/qtrpdf/r_qt1706b.htm.
31. BlackRock, "Company Overview," http://ir.blackrock.com/Cache/1500111836.PDF?O=PDF&T=&Y=&D=&FID=1500111836&iid=4048287; alsoseehttps://www.blackrock.com/institutions/en-ax/literature/newsletter/blackrock-overview-corporate.pdf; also see BlackRock 2016 Investor Day Presentation, http://ir.blackrock.com/Cache/1500088361.PDF?O=PDF&T=&Y=&D=&FID=1500088361&id=4048287; also see Business Insider, https://www.businessinsider.com/blackrock-crushes-earnings-aum-climbs-to-632-trillion-q1-2018-2018-4.
32. The Sovereign Wealth Fund Institute, "Industry Data and Intelligence," https://www.swfinstitute.org/fund-rankings; https://www.swfinstitute.org/sovereign-wealth-fund-rankings/?gclid=Cj0KCQjwlK7cBRCnARIsAJiE3MilDwDZN-0Ua-FqTRHJTTVAOi5f1aaFEkZRV7Z3KLrBh3nl295Uj2saAoH8EALw_wcB.

    Also see "Sovereign Wealth Funds," http://www.economist.com/news/economic-and-financial-indicators/2171362-sovereign-wealth-funds?zid=300&ah=e7b9370e170850b88ef129fa625b13c4.
33. RELX, https://finance.yahoo.com/quote/RELX?p=RELX&.tsrc=fin-srch; John Wiley, https://finance.yahoo.com/quote/JW-A?p=JW-A&.tsrc=fin-srch; Informa PLC, https://finance.yahoo.com/quote/INF.L?p=INF.L&.tsrc=fin-srch.
34. Alfred D. Chandler, *Strategy and Structure: Chapters in the History of the American Industrial Enterprise* (Cambridge, MA: MIT Press, 1995), 1–7, 283–309, 380–393.
35. Peter F. Drucker, *Management: Tasks, Responsibilities, and Practices* (New York: Harper & Row, 1975), 1–27, 58–73, 610–618, 638–782.
36. Michael E. Porter, "The Five Competitive Forces That Shape Strategy," *Harvard Business Review* 86, 1 (January 2008): 78–93.
37. Wolters Kluwer, *2017 Annual General Meeting of Shareholders,* April 20, 2017, http://wolterskluwer.com/binaries/content/assets/wk/pdf/investors/presentations/2017-04-02-wolters-kluwer-agm-2017-presentation.pdf.

38. Vincent Lariviere, Stefanie Haustein, and Philippe Mongeon, "The Oligopoly of Academic Publishers in the Digital Era," *PloS One* 10, 6 (2015): e0127502, 3–16. Also see Elin B. Christianson, "Mergers in the Publishing Industry: 1958–1970," *Journal of Library History* 7, 1 (January 1972): 5–32; and *UC Berkeley Faculty Conference on Scholarly Publishing,* http://www.lib.berkeley.edu/scholarlypublishing/publishiong_models.html.
39. RELX, https://www.elsevier.com/about/policies/pricing; https://www.journals.elsevier.com/brain-research; https://www.elsevier.com/journals/institutional/brain-research/0006-8993.
40. Dave Bogart, ed., *The Bowker Annual: Library and Book Trade Almanac,* 50th ed. (Medford, NJ: Information Today, 2005), 503–504; Dave Bogart, ed., *Library and Book Trade Almanac,* 53rd ed. (Medford, NJ: Information Today, 2008), 515–516; Dave Bogart, ed., *Library and Book Trade Almanac,* 57th ed. (Medford, NJ: Information Today, 2012), 510–511; Dave Bogart, ed., *Library and Book Trade Almanac,* 60th ed. (Medford, NJ: Information Today, 2015), 440–443.
41. Lutz Bornmann and Ruediger Mutz, "Growth Rates of Modern Science: A Bibliometric Analysis Based on the Number of Publications and Cited References," https://arXiv.org/abs/1402.4578.
42. Ware and Mabe, *The STM Report: An Overview of Scientific and Scholarly Journal Publishing 2015,* 6–11.
43. Deni Auclair, *Open Access 2015: Market Size, Forecast, and Trends*, 7–10, http://www.casalini.it/retreat/2015_docs/auclair.pdf.
44. Ibid., Also see Ware and Mabe, *The STM Report: An Overview of Scientific and Scholarly Journal Publishing 2015*, 6–7.
45. Association of American Publishers, *2013 AAP Journals Publishing Survey* (New York: Association of American Publishers, 2015), 2–4, http://publishers.org/sites/default/files/uploads/psp_executive_directors_desk_article-2013.pdf.
46. Copyright Law of the United States and Related Laws Contained in Title 17 of the United States Code; see §302 Duration of Copyright: Works Created After January 1, 1978; see §302(a) (a) IN GENERAL.—Copyright in a work created on or after January 1, 1978, subsists from its creation and, except as provided by the following subsections, endures for a term consisting of the life of the author and 70 years after the author's death. §302 (b) JOINT WORKS.—In the case of a joint work prepared by two or more authors who did not work for hire, the copyright endures for a term consisting of the life of the last surviving author and 70 years after such last surviving author's death; at https://www.copyright.gov/title17/title17.pdf.
47. John Wiley journals, http://www.wileyopenaccess.com/details/content/12f25e0654f/Publication-Charges.html.

48. PloS journals, http://journals.plos.org/plosone/s/publiocation-fees.
49. John Holdren, "Expanding Public Access to the Results of Federally Funded Research," February 22, 2013, https://obamawhitehouse.archives.gov/blog/2013/02/22/expanding-public-access-results-federally-funded-research. Also see the Finch Report, "Report of the Working Group on Expanding Access to Published Research Findings—The Finch Group," https://www.acu.ac.uk/research-information-network/finch-report; Devin Coldewey. "EU Mandates Open Access for All Publicly Funded Research by 2020," https://www.techcrunch.com/2016/05/27/eu-mandates-open-access-for-all-publicly-funded-research-by-2020; also see EU, http://ec.europa.eu/research/participants/docs/h2020-funding-guide/cross-cutting-issues/open-access-data-management/open-access_en.htm; http://ec.europa.eu/research/openscience/index.cfm?pg=openaccess.
50. Economics journals, https://www.researchgate.net/publication/282941581_Submission-demand_in_core_economics_journals_A_panel_study. For information about publication fees, see American Association for Cancer Research, "Information for Authors," http://aacrjournals.org/content/authors/ifora; http://aacrjournals.org/content/authors/select-aacr-journal.
51. Research4Life, http://www.research4life.org: "Research4Life is the collective name for the four programmes that provide developing countries with free or low-cost access to academic and professional peer-reviewed content online. Eligible libraries and their users benefit from: online access to up to 77,000 peer-reviewed international scientific journals, books, and databases; full-text articles which can be downloaded for saving, printing or reading on screen; searching by keyword, subject, author or language; resources available in several languages; and training in information literacy and promotional support.

    Research4Life is a public-private partnership of the World Health Organization (WHO), the United Nation Environment Program (UNEP), the World Intellectual Property Organization (WIPO), Cornell and Yale Universities, the International Association of Scientific, Technical & Medical Publishers, and up to 185 international scientific publishers. The goal of Research4Life is to reduce the knowledge gap between high-income countries and low- and middle-income countries by providing affordable access to critical scientific research. Since 2002, the four programmes—Research in Health (Hinari), Research in Agriculture (AGORA), Research in the Environment (OARE) and Research for Development and Innovation (ARDI)—have provided researchers at more than 8200 institutions in more than 115 low- and middle-income countries with free or low-cost online access to up to 77,000 leading journals and books in the fields of health, agriculture, environment, and applied sciences."

52. Alok Jha, "Academic Spring: How an Angry Maths Blog Sparked a Scientific Revolution," *The Guardian*, April 9, 2012, http://www.theguardian.com/science/2012/apr/09/frustrated-blogpost-boycott-scientific-journals.

[3]

THE PROMOTION AND PLACEMENT OF SCHOLARLY JOURNALS

INTRODUCTION: THE CHANGING STRATEGIES TO PROMOTE SCHOLARLY JOURNALS

Since at least the 1980s, there have been significant changes in the marketing of scholarly journals utilized by the majority of scholarly publishers. This shift meant that traditional advertising (which was very effective for many decades) and direct mail pieces (which were rather ineffective because of 1.5% to 2.0% response rates) were de-emphasized but not eliminated completely. They were supplanted somewhat by the growing use of social media (e.g., Facebook, Twitter) and email.[1]

However, a plethora of other strategies were introduced and adopted, albeit slowly. One new strategy involved the use of metadata, which is, quite simply, data about data; it became an important promotion strategy utilized by journals. Metadata included the traditional library card catalog system; it was a basic five-inch-by-three-inch card that listed information about the author, title, subject, date of publication, publisher, ISBN, number of pages, Library of Congress number or the Dewey Decimal number for the book, and so forth. This card system was replaced in many libraries by the online public access catalog (known as OPAC in libraries), and most libraries removed their card and file boxes when computers were adopted. The Library of Congress (LC) has all of its historic library cards and file boxes, including cards back to about 1800, housed in a massive basement in the Jefferson Library.

Metadata standards have been developed by international organizations, including the American National Standards Institute (ANSI) and the National Information Standards Organization (NISO).[2] The majority of journals adopted metadata systems to ensure that potential readers could discover a specific journal article. A typical metadata includes the following: "(a) descriptive metadata: for finding and understanding a resource, including author, title, subject, genre, publication date; (b) administrative metadata-technical metadata, preservation metadata, and rights metadata: for decoding and rendering files, long-term management of files, and intellectual property rights; (c) structural metadata: relationships of parts of resources to one another; and (d) markup language: integrates metadata and flags for other structural or semantic features within content."[3]

JOURNAL CITATION INDICES

For more than 354 years, journal authors, editors, and publishers had an incomplete understanding of who read a journal since their knowledge was based on the subscription records of society members and libraries and the citation of an article in another article or a book. All of this changed in 1960 when Dr. Eugene Garfield founded the Institute for Scientific Information (ISI); he created (1) the Science Citation Index (now called the Web of Science) in 1964; (2) the internationally known Journal Impact Metrics in 1965, and 1965 was ironically the 300th anniversary of the first journal; (3) the Journal Citation Reports in 1975; and (4) the Arts and Humanities Index in 1978.[4]

Garfield's indices changed the way academics, researchers, and scholarly journals were evaluated. For the first time, a journal's impact factor, as indicated by the ISI citation index, could be measured using a complex formula, and the quest for prestige by authors—that is, publishing an article in a top-tier, high-impact journal—became the measure of success for hiring, tenure, promotion, merit pay, and research grants. However, many researchers seemed to forget the fact that Garfield's indices were an indicator of a journal's impact, not the impact of a specific journal article.

For example, the five top scientific, technical, and medical (STM) scholarly journals, as of June 2018, with high citation indices, based on data on the journal's website, are *CA: A Cancer Journal for Clinicians*, 244.585; *New England Journal of Medicine*, 79.258; *Lancet*, 53.254; *Chemical Reviews*, 52.613; and *Nature Reviews Materials*, 51.941. Journals in the humanities and the social sciences (HSS) category have lower citation indices, for example, *American Historical Review*, 2.615; *Journal of Accounting and Economics*, 2.724; *Journal of Comparative Economics*, 1.170; *Journal of Consumer Psychology*, 2.243; and *Journal of Economic Theory*, 1.033.

Another useful metric is the Scopus Source Normalized Impact per Paper (SNIP), which measures the impact of a paper within a subject field.

However, criticism developed about the use of journal indices as a factor, and in many instances the most important factor, in the hiring, tenure, promotion, and merit pay system that was implemented at most major research universities and scientific research institutions in their quest for prestige. The "invisible hand" of Max Weber's writings on status and social stratification was evident in the never-ending pursuit for higher citation rankings, grant requests, and recognition as a top university in the well-publicized rankings released by *U.S. News* or *The Times Higher Education*.[5]

Stephen Curry, a cell biologist in the United Kingdom, summed up the intrinsic problems of modern scholarship in two rather simple laws. "First law: To get maximum credit for your work, publish in a journal with a high impact factor. Second law: For maximum speed of publication, choose a well-run mega-journal with 'objective' peer review or, better yet, a preprint repository."[6] John Bohannon maintained that "*Nature*, for example, currently has a JIF [journal impact factor] of 41.456, which is generally interpreted to mean that, over the past 2 years, *Nature* articles have been cited, on average, about 41 times each. . . . But for the articles published in any given journal, the distribution of citations is highly skewed. A small fraction of influential papers get most of the citations. . . . So, the average number of citations is often highly misleading."[7]

Vincent Lariviere, Veronique Kiermer, Catriona MacCallum, Marcia McNutt, Mark Patterson, Bernd Pulverer, Sowmya Swaminathan, Stuart Taylor, and Stephen Curry also criticized the extensive use of impact factors because it is "calculated inappropriately as the arithmetic mean of a highly skewed distribution of citations. . . . It is quoted to a higher level of precision (three decimal places) than is warranted by the underlying data; it is based on a narrow two-year time window that is inappropriate for many disciplines; and takes no account of the large variation in citation levels across disciplines."[8] Other scholars expressing concerns about these indices include Masood Fooladi, Hadi Salehi, Melor Yunus, Maryam Farhadi, Arezoo Aghadi Chadegani, Hadi Farahi, and Nader Ale Ebrahim;[9] Vincent Lariviere and Rodrigo Costas;[10] Inder M. Verma;[11] Tobias Kiesslich, Silke B. Weineck, and Dorothea Koelblinger;[12] John Mingers and Liying Yang;[13] and Thed van Leeuwen.[14]

Despite the criticism against the citation index, Garfield's trendsetting work caught the attention of information scientists and corporations who created competing citation indices. Some other important citation indices include Google Scholar, Microsoft Academic Search, Scopus (Elsevier), and Semantic Scholar.[15]

Yet the impact factor remained the "coin of the realm," and a very valuable "coin." Garfield sold ISI to what became Thomson Reuters, and Thomson Reuters issued a series of documents addressing some of the concerns about the impact factor.[16] When Thomson Reuters decided to leave the intellectual property and science sectors to concentrate on other business units, they sold the operations in 2016 for $3.55 billion, including ISI and the Web of Science, to Onex Corporation and Baring Private Equity Asia; the new entity was called Clarivate Analytics.[17]

JOURNAL HOSTING PLATFORMS

In addition to these important developments, a number of influential scholarly journal hosting platforms were created, including Science Direct, JStor, Project Muse, and Highwire; these platforms generated invaluable data for publishers and authors.[18]

Project Muse is a good example of an important hosting journal platform:

> It is a leading provider of digital humanities and social sciences content; since 1995, its electronic journal collections have supported a wide array of research needs at academic, public, special, and school libraries worldwide. Muse books and journals, from leading university presses and scholarly societies, are fully integrated for search and discovery. . . . Project Muse currently includes: 443,437 articles and 1,105,002 chapters by 260 publishers.[19]

The following illustrates the ability of the Project Muse hosting platform to provide immensely useful metadata for authors and publishers about the *Journal of Scholarly Publishing*, a University of Toronto journal.

> *Journal of Scholarly Publishing*. Vol. 35 (2003) through current issue Vol. 50 Number 1 (January 2019). *The Journal of Scholarly Publishing* addresses the age-old problems in publishing as well as the new challenges resulting from changes in technology and funding. Some articles suggest ways to get effectively published

> in books and journals, while others address such topics as editorial and publishing policy, computer applications, electronic publishing, effective marketing and business management. In serving the wide-ranging interests of the international academic publishing community, Journal of Scholarly Publishing provides a balanced look at the issues and concerns—from solutions to the everyday problems to commentary on the philosophical questions at large.
>
> Published by: University of Toronto Press
>
> - Available Issues
> - Search Journal
> - Journal Information

Detailed search capabilities were offered for this journal as well as all the other journals on the Project Muse platform.

SOCIAL COLLABORATION AND SOCIAL SHARING NETWORKS

In the last few years, social collaboration networks (SCNs) and social sharing networks (SSN) were developed and used within academe, including Academia.edu, Altmetrics, Kudos, Mendeley, ResearchGate, and the highly publicized ResearchGate.[20]

ResearchGate is an SCN and SSN; Goldman Sachs and Bill Gates are investors in this site. It provided the following information about its goals and mission:

> ResearchGate is built by scientists, for scientists. It started when two researchers discovered first-hand that collaborating with a friend or colleague on the other side of the world was no easy task. Founded in 2008 . . . ResearchGate today has more than +15 million members. . . . Our mission is to connect the world of

> science and make research open to all. Share your publications, access millions more, and publish your data. Connect and collaborate with colleagues, peers, co-authors, and specialists in your field.[21]

While these statements are reasonable, ResearchGate also contacts researchers, and the web operation often requests that certain journal articles written by a researcher be submitted to ResearchGate because, as indicated in a recent email addressed to a researcher, "You have 8 open full-text requests. View requests."[22] What may not be reasonable is the fact that the researcher may have transferred (and indeed did transfer) the copyright (the list of articles mentioned specifically in this email) to journal publishers, potentially creating a copyright infringement situation for the researcher who sends an article for posting at ResearchGate.

OTHER DATA COLLECTION SITES

SCImago also provides excellent data for researchers and publishers. Its website includes the following information:

> The SCImago Journal & Country Rank is a publicly available portal that includes the journals and country scientific indicators developed from the information contained in the Scopus® database (Elsevier B.V.). . . . Country rankings may also be compared or analyzed separately. Journals can be grouped by subject area (27 major thematic areas), subject category (313 specific subject categories) or by country. Citation data is drawn from over 21,500 titles from more than 5,000 international publishers and country performance metrics from 239 countries worldwide. The SJCR allows you also to embed significant journal metrics into your web as a clickable image widget.[23]

SCImago and many other data-generating sites are superb examples of acquiring actual usage and downloadable data instead of relying only on citation indexes. With them a publisher has a better understanding of what a library needs for its collection, which assists the publisher in crafting a pricing contract. And the library also has hard, reliable data on what journals and articles the library needs to satisfy faculty members and students in their pursuit of scholarship. The irony is that, in academe, the demand from the paying customer (primarily libraries) is driven by faculty, and to a degree from graduate students, which often results in a mostly inelastic demand curve.[24]

RESEARCH REPOSITORIES

A large number of academic libraries and research centers launched institutional repositories, which also generated sizable amounts of data usage patterns. For example, the "Big Ten" universities launched the Big Ten Academic Alliance Open Access Repositories.

> Almost all Big Ten Academic Alliance university libraries manage secure repositories for digital content. While the scope of content held in such repositories varied considerably from university to university, some of the country's largest and best institutional repositories for research findings are maintained by Big Ten Academic Alliance Universities including: the University of Michigan: Deep Blue at the University of Michigan; and University of Michigan Library Repository.[25]

These hosting platforms and institutional repositories highlight the importance of knowing your customer and what the customer wants to read and download, and making sure the library has access to these documents.

BACKLASH

Unfortunately, the law of unforeseen consequences emerged with the emphasis on scholarly output. Jevin D. West, Jennifer Jacquet, Molly M. King, Shelly J. Correll, and Carl T. Bergstrom conducted a research study of more than 8 million research papers across the natural sciences, the social sciences, and the humanities, and they collected gender authorship data between 1990 and 2011 for certain academic disciplines for female authors. The authorship results in their analysis for female journal authors were as follows: mathematics: 10.64% were written by women; philosophy: 12.04%; economics: 13.68%; probability and statistics: 18.11%; political science and international relations: 19.07%; political science and domestic issues: 19.09%; organization and marketing: 25.44%; molecular and cell biology: 29.25%; history: 30.47%; classical studies: 28.88%; cognitive science: 32.12%; anthropology: 36.46%; sociology: 41.41%; demography: 41.90%; and education: 46.35%.[26] While West, Jacquet, King, Correll, and Bergstrom pointed out that progress had been made for female academics, a concerted effort on the part of journal editors, associate and assistant editors, and publishers is needed to make sure that the academic "playing ground" is level for every academic.

Another major concern centers on the bundling of digital and print journals into what has been called the "Big Deal," and its inevitable impact on library budgets (known as the "serials crisis"). The "Big Deal" triggered a number of jeremiads and articles. The University of California, Santa Barbara, presented a widely publicized presentation entitled "Secrets of the 'Big Deal': The Pricing of Academic Journals and the Fleecing of University Libraries."[27] Theodore C. Bergstrom, Paul N. Courant, R. Preston McAfee, and Michael A. Williams analyzed the mean bundle prices by institution type in 2013; their findings indicated significant differences for STM journals from nonprofit society publishers and for-profit publishers.[28]

CONSOLIDATION IN SCHOLARLY JOURNAL PUBLISHING

Concerns emerged about the consolidation in the commercial scholarly publishing sector and the potential impact of these mergers and acquisitions on journal prices. Kathleen Robertson wrote that "the mergers and acquisitions (M & A) most discussed at astronomy meetings are those involving colliding galaxies. However, a major economic change in the ownership of scientific-technical-medical publishing is impacting astronomy information resources, and mergers and acquisitions are the main components of that change."[29] Consolidation in the commercial scholarly publishing sector triggered analyses by Bornmann and Ruediger,[30] Rebecca Trager,[31] and Carolyn E. Lipscomb.[32]

PUBLISHER BOYCOTTS

There have been boycotts of certain commercial scholarly publishers because of the high costs of journal subscriptions. An example includes the Cost of Knowledge, which is a protest organization of academics against the business practices of a specific academic journal publisher. Among the reasons for the protests were a call for lower prices for journals and to promote increased open access to information. The Cost of Knowledge posted the following on the organization's website. The name of the publisher has been deleted and replaced by "X":

> 16,764 Researchers Taking a Stand. Academics have protested X's business practices for years with little effect. These are some of their objections. They charge exorbitantly high prices for subscriptions to individual journals. In the light of these high prices, the only realistic option for many libraries is to agree to buy very large "bundles," which will include many journals that

> those libraries do not actually want. X thus makes huge profits by exploiting the fact that some of their journals are essential. They support measures such as SOPA (Stop Online Piracy Act), PIPA (Protect IP Act) . . . that aim to restrict the free exchange of information. . . . The key to all these issues is the right of authors to achieve easily-accessible distribution of their work. If you would like to declare publicly that you will not support any X journal unless they radically change how they operate, then you can do so by filling in your details on this page.[33]

This organization and its supporters have received the support of many organizations and a few nations, and it is likely that this boycott will continue for quite some time.

OPEN ACCESS

Academics need access to scholarly journals, and since the cost of journals increased, the movement toward gold open access (OA) journals was an almost inevitable response to the "serials crisis." Interest in gold OA journals picked up momentum with the San Francisco Declaration on Research Assessment (DORA; which addressed scholarly outputs) and the Berlin 12 Conference (which called for a migration away from paywall journals toward gold OA journals).[34] In spite of a plethora of academic conferences and research studies lamenting the state of scholarly publications behind paywalls, the launch of the Initiative for Open Citations (I4OC: "a collaboration between scholarly publishers, researchers, and other interested parties to promote the unrestricted availability of scholarly citation data. . . . The aim of this initiative is to promote the availability of data on citations that are structured, separable, and open. Structured means the data representing each publication and each citation instance are expressed in common, machine-readable formats, and that these data can be accessed programmatically.

Separable means the citation instances can be accessed and analyzed without the need to access the source bibliographic products [such as journal articles and books] in which the citations are created. Open means the data are freely accessible and reusable),[35] and the development of the Directory of Open Access Journals (DOAJ), which listed more than 12,000 OA journals and more than 3.66 million articles from 129 countries,[36] for a number of years questions remained unanswered about the future and importance of gold OA journals. When will gold OA journals replace completely traditional "paywall" journals? And when will departmental hiring, tenure, and promotion committees, as well as university administrators, accept gold OA journals as a replacement for high-impact journals in their quest for prestige?

A cluster of important European organizations and a few major funding organizations mandated that research receiving their funding had to appear in gold OA journals, including the Bill and Melinda Gates Foundation and the Wellcome Trust. The Gates Foundation's open access policy is as follows:

> Our Open Access policy contains the following elements: Publications Are Discoverable and Accessible Online. Publications will be deposited in a specified repository(s) with proper tagging of metadata. Publication Will Be On "Open Access" Terms. All publications shall be published under the Creative Commons Attribution 4.0 Generic License (CC BY 4.0) or an equivalent license. This will permit all users of the publication to copy and redistribute the material in any medium or format and transform and build upon the material, including for any purpose (including commercial) without further permission or fees being required. Foundation Will Pay Necessary Fees. The foundation would pay reasonable fees required by a publisher to effect publication on these terms. Publications Will Be Accessible and Open Immediately. All publications shall be available immediately upon their publication, without

> any embargo period. An embargo period is the period during which the publisher will require a subscription or the payment of a fee to gain access to the publication. We are, however, providing a transition period of up to two years from the effective date of the policy (or until January 1, 2017). During the transition period, the foundation will allow publications in journals that provide up to a 12-month embargo period. Data Underlying Published Research Results Will Be Accessible and Open Immediately. The foundation will require that data underlying the published research results be immediately accessible and open. This too is subject to the transition period and a 12-month embargo may be applied.[37]

Yet the movement toward gold OA was rather slow, which prompted many industry observers to believe that, at some point, gold OA journals would prevail[38] but that it would be a long time before the major research universities in North America, Europe, and the rest of the world modify their well-established pilgrimage toward global rankings.

COALITION S AND PLAN S

However, all of this changed on September 4, 2018. The cOAlition S plan, generally called Plan S, was released by 11 funders, which included the national funding agencies in the United Kingdom, the Netherlands, and France, along with Italy's National Institute for Nuclear Physics. The terms and conditions of Plan S are rather complex and, in some instances, convoluted:

> Plan S is an initiative for Open Access publishing that was launched in September 2018. The plan is supported by cOAlition S, an international consortium of research funders. Plan S requires that, from [January 1] 2020, scientific publications that

result from research funded by public grants must be published in compliant Open Access journals or platforms.[39]

cOAlition S provides "guidance" on the implementation of Plan S:

Aim and Scope Plan S aims for full and immediate Open Access to publications from publicly funded research. The coalition of research funders that have committed to implement Plan S, known as cOAlition S, therefore calls for a definitive shift towards new models of academic publishing. cOAlition S aims to accelerate the transition to a scholarly publishing system that is characterized by immediate, free online access to, and largely unrestricted use and re-use of scholarly publications. cOAlition S recognizes that research funders, institutions, researchers, learned societies, librarians, and publishers must work together towards a system of scholarly publishing that is more accessible, efficient, fair, and transparent. cOAlition S will also promote a culture that ensures that young scholars have opportunities to excel and advance their careers. cOAlition S is committed to fulfil the specific target set out in Plan S—immediate Open Access to all scholarly publications from research funded by coalition members from 2020 onwards. cOAlition S does not favor any specific business model for Open Access publishing or advocate any particular route to Open Access given that there should be room for new innovative publishing models. Plan S applies to all scholarly output that is reviewed according to accepted standards within relevant disciplines and is based on results from research funded fully or partially by cOAlition S members. In addition, cOAlition S strongly encourages that research data, preprints, and other research outputs are made openly accessible, subject to the usual legal and ethical considerations. cOAlition S supports the intentions of the San Francisco Declaration on Research Assessment (DORA) that research needs to be assessed on its own merits rather than on the basis of the venue in which the research is published. cOAlition S members intend to sign DORA and implement those requirements in their policies.[40]

Regarding the implementation of Plan S, cOAlition S released the following statement:

> All scholarly articles that result from research funded by members of cOAlition S must be openly available immediately upon publication without any embargo period. They must be permanently accessible under an open license allowing for re-use for any purpose, subject to proper attribution of authorship. cOAlition S recommends using Creative Commons licenses (CC) for all scholarly publications and will by default require the CC BY Attribution 4.0 license for scholarly articles. Scholarly articles are compliant with Plan S if they are published in compliant Open Access journals or on compliant Open Access platforms. In addition, cOAlition S will, under specified conditions, accept deposit of scholarly articles in Open Access repositories and, in a transition period, publishing Open Access in subscription journals ("hybrid Open Access") under transformative agreements as means to achieve compliance with Plan S. Open Access journals or Open Access platforms: deposition of scholarly articles in Open Access repositories; transformative agreements; Authors publish in a Plan S compliant Open Access journal or on a Plan S compliant Open Access platform with a CC BY license. Immediately upon publication, authors deposit the final published version of a scholarly publication (Version of Record; VoR) or an Author's Accepted Manuscript (AAM), in a Plan S compliant repository. The document is made available immediately [as] open access (with no embargo) under a CC BY license. Authors publish Open Access with a CC BY license in a subscription journal that is covered by a transformative agreement that has a clear and time-specified commitment to a full Open Access transition.[41]

THE RESPONSE OF THE RESEARCH COMMUNITY TO PLAN S

Important components of the research community responded rather quickly to cOAlition S's announcement. For example, the Gates Foundation, the Wellcome Trust, the Chinese government, Harvard University, the Conference of Open Access Repositories (COAR), and many other entities enthusiastically supported Plan S. There was a mass resignation of the entire editorial board of *Informetrics*, and these editors launched a new competing gold OA journal called *Quantitative Science Studies*. MIT Press announced in January 2019 that it would publish this new OA journal, "with an editorial board of well-known OA scholars."[42]

Other individuals questioned the wisdom of Plan S, others called it a "risky" strategy that could impact negatively scientific research for researchers not able to obtain grants to cover APCs (article processing charges), and still others wondered if it would be accepted in the humanities or even in the United States.[43]

COALITION S AND PLAN S: A WORK IN PROGRESS

Plan S is a major inflection point in the long history of scholarly journals. In essence, journals, including some of the major STM journals (e.g., *Nature, Science, Cell,* etc.) would have to change their basic business model to accommodate the terms of Plan S and discontinue paywalls. This means that a journal's numerous managerial obligations (e.g., manuscript review, contacting peer reviewers, responding to authors and peer reviewers, line editing, and production, including art, design, layout, and page make-up) and the production of printed journals and the posting of journals on websites would have to rely on APCs, advertisements, conferences, submission fees, page and other publication charges, etc., to finance their operations and obligations (e.g., insurance, information technology systems, pay and benefits, rent or mortgages, utilities, taxes, etc.). However, it appears that cOAlition S might seek to put a "cap" (i.e., the maximum amount a journal could charge) on APC charges, which could dampen this revenue stream. On the horizon, cOAlition S might add scholarly books to their list of scholarly publications. Clearly, cOAlition S is a policy in progress. Many questions remain about whether cOAlition S's mandated requirements will be accepted in the United States, the largest market for scholarly communications in the world.

JOURNAL VALUE CHAIN

What is the value chain in the scholarly journal sector? Assume a faculty member is interested in writing a business history research article on the decision of Westinghouse to launch a radio station in 1920. The faculty member starts with a review of the published history of Westinghouse and the radio industry, which can take several months; it can take longer if the researcher needs access to archives. The researcher discovers that in 1920 Westinghouse was one of the major radio manufacturers in the United States. However, in 1920 there were no commercial radio stations, which prompted Westinghouse, on November 2, 1920, to launch KDKA, the nation's first commercial radio station. It was the first radio station to broadcast the election results of the 1920 presidential election, sports, religious programs, talk shows, and news. The success of KDKA sparked interest in creating radio stations in New York City, Chicago, and other cities; by 1924 there were more than 600 radio stations in the United States. Today, KDKA is still in business operating both AM (ranked eighth by Nielsen Audio Ratings) and FM (ranked fifth) radio operations; in 1920 there was only AM radio.

The researcher spends about three to six months writing the article, including detailed technical and economic information about the initial success of KDKA as well as data about the impact the station had on listeners in Pittsburgh and western Pennsylvania. After the researcher checks the facts and the journal's required style manual and prepares a conflict of interest statement, he sends the documents to a journal, perhaps *Business History* (an Oxford University Press journal).

The editor or perhaps the associate editor or an area editor (often called the supervising editor) reviews the article, ascertains the article has merit, and sends it to three peer reviewers for analysis. The reviewers have about 45 days to analyze the article, and they forward their recommendations to the journal's editor. Their collective decision is a "revise and resubmit." This information is collected and sent by the editor supervising the submission as an email to the author, who decides to follow the detailed recommendations of the reviewers.

After about two or three months, the supervising editor receives the revised article with a detailed narrative from the author stipulating clearly how each recommendation was incorporated into the revised article. The editor sends the peer reviewers the revised article and the author's detailed narrative. After about 45 days, the reviewers inform the editor that the article, with all of the recommendations, is acceptable for publication. The editor sends an email to the author informing him of the journal's decision to publish the article, and a contract is attached to the editor's email. The author reviews, signs, and returns the contract to the editor.

Once a signed contract is received by the journal, the following processes start: editorial, art, design, layout, and page make-up, which includes setting the type for the article. The supervising editor, or perhaps the journal's line editor, reviews the page proofs and sends the page proofs as an email attachment, generally with a series of "author queries" (known as AQs), to the author, who is asked to review carefully and return the proofs in 10 days. The author is instructed to identify any printing errors (known as PEs); for example, perhaps the word "behavior" was spelled incorrectly by the typesetter. The author is also notified that a very limited number of "author's alterations"

(AAs) can be listed on the page proofs; if an "excessive" number of AAs are submitted, the author can be charged a fee.

After the revised page proofs are evaluated at the journal, the article is generally sent to the printer and also posted on the journal's website. Individuals with access to, for example, Project Muse will have access to the complete posted article. Individuals who lack access to a Project Muse website can purchase the article for a fee, which can vary significantly between STM journals and HSS journals. The revenue stream from Project Muse or other websites, as well as paid subscriptions, subrights, etc., accrues to the journal; the author receives nothing for the time and effort to research and write the article.

Of course, this was a positive outcome for the author. Unfortunately, the rejection rate at top journals, and *Business History* is a major journal, can range between 90% and 95%. A rejected article may be sent to another journal, with perhaps a rejection rate in the 75% range, increasing the possibility of publication and rewarding the author for months of researching, writing, and revising. The alternative, which happens all too frequently, is that the article is never published, collecting dust in a file cabinet.

A JOURNAL CONTRACT

Academics and researchers have a mastery of their academic field(s). However, many of them do not have a firm grasp of contract law or copyright law, and paywall scholarly journal publishers insist that an author sign an agreement to transfer the copyright from the author to the publisher.

The following is a typical scholarly journal contract between a journal and an author. Most of the terms and conditions are standard contract language, often called "boilerplate" by some in publishing. Relevant material from the Copyright Law of the United States, 17 U.S.C., is included to highlight certain issues raised in the contract.[44]

The Contract and Analysis

AUTHOR(S): ABC

ADDRESS: DEF

The University of GHI (GHI) Press is pleased to have the privilege of publishing your contribution to *GHI* entitled "JKL."

Item #1. GHI will perform the usual functions of copy-editing on the article. The Author(s) will be given an opportunity to read and correct proofs, but if they fail to return them by the date set on the proofs, production and publication may proceed without the Author(s)'s approval of proofs.

Item #2. GHI will publish this article pursuant to this contract at its cost. GHI has the exclusive right to determine how the article will appear in the journal and elsewhere.

Item #3. The Author(s) warrant that permission to publish the article has not been previously assigned elsewhere. The Author(s) further warrant that the contribution is original to them, except for any copyrighted material of others incorporated in it, and that the Author(s) will advise us of any material, either text or illustration, the rights for which are controlled by others. Where necessary, the Author(s) will obtain, before publication and at their expense, permission in writing from the owner of the copyright in that material for publication by us. Copies of any such permission must be submitted to GHI for our files.

Item #4. The Author(s) further warrant that the article contains no defamatory or otherwise unlawful matter and that it makes no improper invasion of the privacy or personal rights of anyone. The Author(s) undertake that all statements in it purporting to be facts are true; and that they will advise us of any statements that might be construed as defamatory or otherwise unlawful. We may require substantive revision of the manuscript to avoid including material that may infringe rights or be defamatory or otherwise unlawful.

Item #5. In the unlikely event of any claim, action, or proceeding based on an alleged violation of any of these warranties, we shall have the right to defend the same through counsel of our own choosing.

The Author(s) agree to pay all resulting costs and damages, except that this indemnity shall not apply to any changes in the manuscript by us that were not approved by the Author(s) in advance of publication, or to any material that the Authors had warned us in advance of publication might be construed as defamatory or otherwise unlawful.

Item #6. In order to protect both Author(s) and GHI from unauthorized use of the article, the Author(s) agree to refer to us any subsequent requests to publish it or a substantial portion thereof. If we choose to grant any such request, we will normally exact a standard fee for reprinting, the amount of this fee to be fixed by us from time to time; this fee will be divided equally with Author(s). We will accede to any request by the Author(s) to use part or all of their article in a larger work published under either Author(s)' exclusive authorship or editorship, provided that acknowledgment of its first appearance is made in a manner approved by UTP, and in such cases no fee for reprinting shall be payable to us.

Item #7. Subject to the above conditions, and in consideration of GHI undertaking to subsidize costs of publication of the article, the Author(s) assign to GHI the exclusive world rights to the article in its present, or substantially its present form, and the parties hereto agree upon the foregoing terms for themselves and their respective executors, administrators, assigns, or successors. The Author(s) hereby waive any claim for royalties arising from the use by GHI of their article. GHI hereby obtains the right to use the article in any future publication, including, but not limited to, publication in electronic media, issued under its auspices and to authorize others, including reproduction rights organizations such as Access Copyright and electronic database providers such as Project Muse, to do the same. The Author(s) hereby grant GHI the nonexclusive right to create the Digital Object Identifier (DOI) for this article and to deposit the DOI with CrossRef, the official DOI registration agency for scholarly and professional publications.

________________________ ________________________

Signature of the Editor Date Signature of Author Date

Analysis of the Contract

The name of the author and his or her address are listed, and this information should be checked carefully if the author is moving to a new university or research institution. The title of the article is listed. Again, make sure that the title is correct.

Item #1 in the contract: The publisher will perform a standard editorial review of the page proofs. However, the author is expected to review these proofs and return them in a timely manner. Failure to adhere to this clause means the publisher will handle the final set of proofs without "the author's approval of proofs," which is clearly not in the best interest of the author.

Item #2 in the contract: While this section is a brief single sentence, it is very important; since copyright of the article is transferred from the author to the publisher under item #7 in this contract (see item #7 in this section), the author grants exclusive rights to the publisher to publish it when it sees fit as well as subsidiary (called "sub") rights and foreign rights—that is, to have it published perhaps in an anthology of articles that appear in a book or in a magazine or is sold to a foreign publisher who will translate it into another language, perhaps Spanish or Chinese. 17 U.S.C. §204 states the following: "execution of transfers of copyright ownership (a) A transfer of copyright ownership, other than by operation of law, is not valid unless an instrument of conveyance, or a note or memorandum of the transfer, is in writing and signed by the owner of the rights conveyed or such owner's duly authorized agent."[45]

Item #3 in the contract: This is a complex section of the contract. The author warrants that the material has not been previously assigned or published elsewhere and is original material; if any copyrighted material was used, the author is obligated to obtain written permission authorizing the use of this material. However, 17 U.S.C. §106 and §107 deal with the concept of "fair use," and every scholar and researcher should be familiar with these two sections of 17 U.S.C. §106 outlines, rather clearly, the fact that the author has exclusive rights over the content.[46] However, §107 addresses the limitations of exclusivity, which allows an author the right, under the "fair use" concept, to use material as long as the terms and conditions of §107 are followed, specifically that "the fair use of a copyrighted work, including such use by reproduction in copies or phonorecords or by any other means specified by that section, for purposes such as criticism, comment, news reporting, teaching (including multiple copies for classroom use), scholarship, or research, is not an infringement of copyright."[47] The author must follow carefully the language of this section, which stipulates

> (1) the purpose and character of the use, including whether such use is of a commercial nature or is for nonprofit educational purposes; (2) the nature of the copyrighted work; (3) the amount and substantiality of the portion used in relation to the copyrighted work as a whole; and (4) the effect of the use upon the potential market for or value of the copyrighted work.[48]

Item #4 in the contract: This section requires the author to stipulate that the article contains no inflammatory or defamatory statements. If the publisher believes the article contains inflammatory or defamatory statements, the publisher can insist that the content be changed to delete any inflammatory or defamatory statements.

Item #5 in the contract: If the author and/or the publisher are involved in any litigation regarding the article, the publisher has the right to hire its own attorney, and the author agrees to pay for any costs and damages related to any litigation unless the litigation centers on changes in the manuscript that were not approved by the author.

Item #6 in the contract: Since the author no longer holds the copyright of the article under the terms of item #7, if the author is contacted by anyone requesting to use all or parts of the article, the author is obligated to notify the publisher; the publisher will attempt to negotiate a fee for use of the material (a subright or a foreign right).

Item #7 in the contract: Since the publisher assumes all costs associated with the preparation, publication, and distribution of the article, the author transfers to the publisher world copyrights, and the publisher, if a US publisher, will hold this copyright for the life of the author and 70 after the death of the author. If the article had more than one author, the copyright will be held for the life of the surviving author and 70 after the death of the second, or third, etc., author. Lastly, the author agrees that the publisher has the right to publish and/or distribute the article in any database provider and/or obtain any registration of the article. These issues are addressed in U.S.C. §201,[49] §201(d),[50] and §302.[51]

The final part of the contract requires the author to sign and date the contract, which will be signed and dated by the publisher upon receipt of the author's copy. A copy of the completed contract, with all the necessary signatures, will be sent to the author, and the original will be retained by the publisher.

ISSUES OF CONCERN ABOUT THE STATE OF SCHOLARLY JOURNAL PUBLISHING

First, many individuals involved in the scholarly journal community have expressed concerns about journals moving around from one publisher to another. However, authors basically have a relationship with a specific journal, not the publisher who handles the back-office operations. There have been some boycotts of a select number of journals and journal publishers. This situation could pose a serious problem if a journal signed with a publisher under a boycott.

Second, many journal observers, including librarians, authors, and university administrators, have concerns about journal subscription costs. One issue centers on a commercial scholarly publisher taking over a journal; raising subscription costs for a single journal and/or creating an economic bundle of journals, known as the "big deal"; and requiring a library to subscribe to the entire bundle. While the average subscription price for a specific journal is often lower in the "big deal," the library is compelled to subscribe to journals that are of little or no interest to faculty members or students.

Third, another major concern centers on the fact that many US university libraries have faced large increases in their journal costs while not experiencing any increase, much less a substantial increase, in their budgets. This issue generated a significant amount of publicity within academic and library circles, including some reports that library subscription costs were unsustainable, and that this conundrum resulted in a reduction in the purchase of scholarly journals.

Fourth, concerns about subscription costs have triggered a global interest in digital journals and gold OA journals, especially access to academics, researchers, and students in developing nations. Digital journals were well received within the academic and research world.[52] Journal articles were posted quickly, articles were available on any computer or tablet that had access to a library or a repository, and access was available 24/7. In most cases, the reader could download and/or print out a copy of the article, although the rise of piracy forced many publishers to adopt a "read-only" access policy (e.g., the *Harvard Business Review*). Almost all journals are disseminated electronically, with print largely reserved for institutional or individual subscribers, many of whom receive it as part of their annual dues for membership in a learned society (e.g., *American Political Science Review*). With digital journals publishers save money on printing, paper, binding, warehousing, and distribution through the mail.

Fifth, the basic arguments for gold OA were rather compelling. A gold OA journal cost the library nothing, effectively freeing the library to decide on purchasing books or other services. Most librarians, and a number of academics and researchers, supported OA, and a few viewed it almost as a moral crusade against commercial scholarly publishers with what were called "high profits," although OA is every bit as much a business response to high commercial publisher pricing.[53]

Sixth, many university presses and commercial scholarly publishers had to change their business models because (1) a number of academic libraries started publishing journals (e.g., the University of Michigan), (2) a large number of governments created requirements that any (nonclassified) article derived from government-funded access had to be made available free of charge (with or without an APC) within a certain time period, and (2) a cluster of foundations (e.g., the Gates Foundation) required that any research support for an article must be made available free of charge.

Seventh, there has been growth in the number of researchers and academics, substantive advances in technology, and an increase in research and development budgets that generally outpaced annual changes in the gross domestic product (GDP). These events impacted the total number of researchers publishing scholarly journal articles and where articles were published. *Nature* reported in December 2018 that "China now publishes more scientific research than the United States."[54] This change could have an impact on national research funding agencies and research and development allocations in the United States and Europe; it is possible that the movement toward Plan S might have an impact on research output. However, a major concern centers on long-term preservation of these articles since traditional libraries might have access only to online access (or whatever replaces online) and not have access to printed journals.

Eighth, the emergence of gold OA "megajournals" (often called OAMI journals) has directly and significantly impacted scholarly journal publishing. Essentially, megajournals (e.g., *PloS One*) have a broader publishing focus and scope than traditional journals; many of the megajournals publish thousands of articles annually with interesting APCs (often topping $5,000.00). While the OAMI journals have an intriguing business model, it remains to be seen whether they can break away from their reputation as a "dumping ground" for articles[55] and modify their models in a cOAlition S and Plan S environment, which has discussed hard "caps" on the amounts of APCs.

Ninth, these developments triggered a response from the vast majority of university presses, academic societies, and commercial scholarly publishers; they modified their business model to include three author options: (1) traditional paywall print journals; (2) hybrid journals, which offered the author the opportunity either to submit the article and transfer the copyright to the publisher or to pay an APC and retain the copyright; and (3) a completely gold OA journal, with an APC. Because of a series of related and unrelated events in the past few decades, scholarly journal publishing is clearly an exceptionally complicated endeavor. For example, academic library annual expenditures of journals (often listed as "serials" or "periodicals and serials" in the published statistical datasets) as a percentage of total library expenditures decreased from 40.44% in 2001 to 22.40% in 2017. It is likely that continued declines in journals' percentage of total expenditures are likely as other pivotal costs for library materials and salaries increase (e.g., "other print materials," manuscripts and archives, audio equipment and materials, microforms, electronic references, preservation costs, salaries and benefits, security, etc.). Table 3.1 lists periodicals and serials data for the years 2001–2017.

In addition, many academic societies are deeply concerned about the potential impact of Plan S on their mission to disseminate scholarly communications.[56] The numerous architects of cOAlition S and Plan S need to create long-term realistic and workable guidelines for the scholarly publishers, authors, libraries, and readers of what has become almost an avalanche of scholarly journals and articles, including addressing the creation of innovative "mirror" journals (i.e., scholarly journals with the same editor and editorial boards as paywall journals) designed to get around the philosophy and goals of Plan S and the gold OA community.[57]

Unfortunately, a number of journals, primarily in the STM sector, were adversely impacted when conflicts of interest emerged, for example, authors receiving paid research support and as a result

Table 3.1 ACADEMIC LIBRARY ACQUISITIONS EXPENDITURES, 2001–2017: PERIODICALS AND SERIALS

Year	*Total Expenditures*	*Periodicals and Serials Expenditures*	*Periodicals and Serials Percent of Total Expenditures*
2001	$1,358,969,601	$549,542,562	40.44%
2002	$1,443,102,475	$577,029,105	39.99%
2003	$1,352,674,991	$512,076,817	37.86%
2004	$1,429,793,005	$566,180,759	39.60%
2005	$1,363,013,834	$525,080,399	38.52%
2006	$739,643,639	$247,086,535	33.41%
2007	$960,876,102	$306,914,207	31.94%
2008	$1,163,695,836	$310,285,323	26.66%
2009	$870,146,267	$235,869,715	27.11%
2010	$1,075,146,358	$319,074,180	29.68%
2011	$1,074,282,010	$316,302,232	29.44%
2012	$1,088,781,751	$302,411,821	27.78%
2013	$1,159,993,119	$299,509,276	25.82%
2014	$1,165,136,885	$278,332,796	23.89%
2015	$1,139,269,827	$249,083,351	21.86%
2016	$1,040,802,593	$230,127,247	22.11%
2017	$942,878,213	$211,216,942	22.40%

N.B. Based on statistical data from various sources. The datasets are for an academic year, so, for example, 2002 represents expenditures for the 2001–2002 academic year. Over the years, the category has been called serials and, at times, periodicals and serials.

Source: *The Bowker Annual* and *The Library and Book Trade Almanac*, various years.

analyzing a company or product positively, but not objectively. This prompted many journal publishers, editors, and editorial boards to insist that authors must submit a signed conflict of interest form when the article is submitted to the journal.[58] While not fool-proof, it represents a good-faith effort of journals to ensure that accurate, and not slanted or inaccurate, information or conclusions are presented.

While the precise terms and conditions for Plan S have yet to be codified and made public, especially regarding the inevitable movement toward a gold OA policy for books, a "variation" of the basic quest toward global OA has been promulgated, called "Plan U," which is a mandated preprint policy for STM articles (although HSS and legal, tax, and regulatory [LTR] journals could be added). The basic parameters of Plan U were announced in February 2019: "Plan U would require immediately archived [and] universal free access to academic research; speed research through earlier and wider dissemination of results; and produce opportunities for new initiatives in peer review and research evaluation."[59]

Key arguments for Plan U were outlined on the Plan U website:

> If all research funders required their grantees to post their manuscripts first on preprint servers—an approach we refer to as "Plan U"—the widespread desire to provide immediate free access to the world's scientific output would be achieved with minimal effort and expense. As noted above, mathematicians, physicists and computer scientists have been relying on arXiv as their primary means of communication for decades. The biomedical sciences were slower to adopt preprinting, but bioRxiv is undergoing exponential growth and several million readers access articles on bioRxiv every month. Depositing preprints is thus increasingly common among scientists, and mandating it would simply accelerate adoption of a process many predict will become universal in the near future. There is a precedent for mandating preprint deposition: since 2017, the Chan Zuckerberg Initiative (CZI) has mandated that all grantees deposit preprints prior to

> or at submission for formal publication. This requirement has been accepted by CZI-funded investigators, many of whom were already routinely depositing manuscripts on bioRxiv.[60]

It remains to be seen if Plan U will have traction to augment Plan S in the foreseeable future.

We live and work in turbulent times. The future of scholarly journal publishing appears to be, at best, a dynamic sector lacking clear managerial and marketing policies as the forces of change impact directly, positively or negatively, what academics do on a daily basis to undertake research and publish their findings.

NOTES

1. Email received on June 21, 2017, from Oxford University Press regarding the *Journal of Consumer Research*, https://mail.google.com/mail/u/0/?tab=wm#search/oxford/15ccaf4524c7174f.
2. American National Standards Institute (ANSI), https://www.ansi.org; National Information Standards Organization (NISO), http://www.niso.org.
3. National Information Standards Organization, *Understanding Metadata: What Is Metadata, and What Is It For?*, http://www.niso.org/apps/group_public/download.php/17446/Understanding%20Metadata.pdf and http://creativecommons.org/licenses/by-ne/4.0/legalcode.
4. Clarivate Analytics, "In Memoriam: Dr. Eugene Garfield September 16, 1925–February 26, 2017," http://clarivate.com/dr-garfield. Also see Eugene Garfield, *Citation Indexing: Its Theory and Application in Science Technology and Humanities* (New York: Wiley-Interscience, 1979), 57–117; Garfield Library, http://garfield.library.upenn.edu; Melinda Baldwin, "Origins of the Journal Impact Factor," *Physics Today*, January 17, 2017, physics-today.scitation.org/do/10.1063/PT.5.9082.
5. Max Weber, "The Distribution of Power Within the Community: Classes, *Stande*, Parties," trans. Dagmar Waters, Tony Waters, Elizabeth Hahnke, Maren Lippke, Eva Ludwig-Gluck, Daniel Mai, Nina Ritzi-Messner, Christina Veldhoen, and Lucas Fassnacht, *Journal of Classical Sociology* 10, 2 (2010): 142–144. Also see Albert N. Greco, "Academic Libraries and the Economics of Scholarly Publishing in the Twentieth-First Century: Portfolio Theory, Product Differentiation, Economic Rent, Perfect Price

Discrimination, and the Cost of Prestige," *Journal of Scholarly Publishing* 47, 1 (October 2015): 1–43. For the ranking of the best US graduate schools by *U.S. News*, see https://www.usnews.com/best-graduate-schools; for the rankings of the top global universities by the *Times Higher Education*, see https://www.timeshighereducation.com/world-university-rankings/2016/world-ranking.

6. Stephen Curry, "Can We Amend the Laws of Scholarly Publishing?," http://occamstypewriter.org/scurry/2015/04/29/amend-laws-scholarly-publication.
7. John Bohannon, "Hate Journal Impact Factors? New Study Gives You One More Reason," *Science*, July 6, 2016, http://www.sciencemag.org/news/2016/07/hate-impact-factors-bew-study-gives-you-one-more-reason.
8. Vincent Lariviere, Veronique Kiermer, Catriona J. MacCallum, Marcia McNutt, Mark Patterson, Bernd Pulverer, Sowmya Swaminathan, Stuart Taylor, and Stephen Curry, "A Simple Proposal for the Publication of Journal Citation Distributions," *BioRxiv*, July 5, 2016, http://www.biorxiv.org/content/early/2016/07/05/062109. Also see Ewen Callaway, "Beat It, Impact Factor! Publishing Elite Turns Against Controversial Metric," *Nature*, July 8, 2016, http://www.nature.com//news/beat-it-impact-factor-publishing-elite-turns-against=controversial-metric-1,20224.
9. Masood Fooladi, Hadi Salehi, Melor Yunus, Maryam Farhadi, Arezoo Aghadi Chadegani, Hadi Farahi, and Nader Ale Ebrahim, "Does Criticisms Overcome the Praises of Journal Impact Factor?," *Canadian Center of Science and Education* 9, 5 (2013): 176–182.
10. Vincent Lariviere and Rodrigo Costas, "How Many Is Too Many? On the Relationships Between Research Productivity and Impact," *PloS One* 11, 9 (2016): e0162709.
11. Inder M. Verma, "Impact, Not Impact Factor," *PNAS* 112, 26 (June 30, 2015): 2875–2876, http://www.pnas.org/cgi/doi/10.1073/pnas.1509912112.
12. Tobias Kiesslich, Silke B. Weineck, and Dorothea Koelblinger, "Reasons for Journal Impact Factor Changes: Influence of Changing Source Items," *PloS One* 11, 4 (2016): e0154199, doi.org/10.1371/journal.pone.0154199. Also see Matthew J. Michalska-Smith and Stefano Allesina, "And, Not Or: Quality, Quantity in Scientific Publishing," *PloS One* 12, 6: e0178074, https://doi.org/10.1371/journal.pone.0178074.
13. John Mingers and Liying Yang, "Evaluating Journal Quality: A Review of Journal Citation Indicators and Ranking in Business and Management," https://arxiv.org/ftp/arxiv/papers/1604/1604.06685.pdf.
14. Thed van Leeuwen, "Discussing Some Basic Critique on Journal Impact Factors: Revision of Some Earlier Comments," *Scientometrics* 92, 2

(August 2012): 443–455, https://www.ncbi.nlm.gov/pmc/articles/PMC3399074.

15. Google Scholar, https://scholar.google.com; Microsoft Academic Search, http://academic.research.microsoft.com; Scopus, https://www.elsevier.com/solutions/scopu; and Semantic Scholar, https://www.semanticscholar.org. Also see Syed Rahmat Ullah Shah, Khalid Mahmood, and Abdul Hameed, "Review of Google Scholar, Web of Science, and Scopus Research Results: The Case of Inclusive Education Research," University of Nebraska, Lincoln Digital Commons, http://digitalcommons.unl.edu/libphilprac.
16. Thomson Reuters, *Journal Impact Factor—Snapshot of a 3 Year Window*, http://anyflip.com/otwt/npjm, http://scientific.thomson.com/wok/media/pdf/Impact_Factor_2016_release.pdf.
17. Clarivate Analytics, "Acquisition of the Thomson Reuters Intellectual Property and Science Business by Onex and Baring Asia Completed," press release, October 3, 2016, http://news.clarivate.com. Also see Bob Grant, "Web of Science Sold for More Than $3 Billion," *The Scientist*, July 15, 2016, http://www.the-scientist.com/?articles.view/articleNo/46558/title/Web-of-Science-Sold-for-More-Than--3-Billion; Thomson Reuters, "Thomson Reuters Announces Definitive Agreement to Sell Its Intellectual Property & Science Business to Onex and Baring Asia for $3.55 Billion," press release, July 11, 2016, https://www.thomsonreuters.com/en/press-releases/2016/july/thomson-reuters-announces-definitive-agreement-to-sell-its-intellectual-property-science-business.html; Christopher King, "Clarivate's Global Institutional Profiles Project Underscores the Importance of Reputation," http://clarivate.com/clarivates-global-institutional-profiles-project-underscores-the-importance-of-reputation/?category=science-research-connent.
18. Science Direct, http://www.sciencedirect.com; JSTOR, https://www.jstor.org; Project Muse, https://muse.jhu.edu; and Highwire, http://home.highwire.org.
19. See Project Muse, https://muse.jhu.edu.
20. Academia.edu, http://www.academia.edu; ACS Chemworx, https://hp.acschemworx.acs.org; Altmetrics, https://www.altmetric.com; Kudos, https://www.growkudos.com; Mendeley, https://www.mendeley.com; ResearchGate, https://www.researchgate.net; SCImago, https://www.scimagojr.com; and the Scopus Source Normalized Impact per Page, http://journalinsights.elsevier.com/journals/0969-806X/snip.
21. ResearchGate, https://www.researchgate.net/about. Also see Ingrid Lunden, "ResearchGate Raises $52.6M [Million] for Its Social Research Network for Scientists," Techcrunch, February 28, 2018, https://techcrunch.com/2017/02/28/researchgate-raises-52-6m-for-

its-social-research-network-for-scientists: "This latest tranche of money comes from an impressive list of strategic and financial investors that include the Wellcome Trust, Goldman Sachs Investment Partners, and Four Rivers Group, Ashton Kutcher, LVMH, Xavier Niel, Bill Gates, Benchmark, and Founders Fund, some of whom (like Gates, Benchmark and Founders Fund) were investors in previous rounds."

22. Email received on January 13, 2019.
23. SCImago, http://www.scimagojr.com/aboutus.php.
24. N. Gregory Mankiw, *Principles of Economics,* 2nd ed. (Fort Worth, TX: Harcourt College Publishers, 1998), 94: "The law of demand states that a fall in the price of a good raises the quantity demanded. The price elasticity of demand measures how much of the quantity demanded responds to a change in price. Demand is said to be elastic if the quantity demanded responds substantially to changes in the price. Demand is said to be inelastic if the quantity demanded responds only slightly to changes in the price." Also see Gadi Fibich, Arieh Gavious, and Oded Lowemgart, "The Dynamics of Price Elasticity of Demand in the Presence of Reference Price Effects," *Journal of the Academy of Marketing Science* 33, 1 (December 2005): 66–78. Albert N. Greco, *The Economics of the Publishing and Information Industries: The Search for Yield in a Disintermediated World* (New York and London: Routledge, 2015), 58–65, 75–77.
25. Big Ten Academic Alliance Open Access Repositories, https://www.btaa.org/projects/library/scholarly-communication/open-access-repositories.
26. The best article outlining the need to understand the consumer is Theodore Levitt, "Marketing Myopia," *Harvard Business Review* 53 (September–October 1975): 26–37. Also see Robert H. Hayes and William J. Abernathy, "Managing Our Way to Economic Decline," *Harvard Business Review* 58 (July–August 1980): 67–77.
27. Jevin D. West, Jennifer Jacquet, Molly M. King, Shelly J. Correll, and Carl T. Bergstrom, "The Role of Gender in Scholarly Authorship," *PloS One* 8, 7 (2013): e66212, https://doi.org/10.1371/journal.pone.0066212. Also see Tracy Vence, "Pondering Science Publishing," *The Scientist*, December 16, 2013, http://www.the-scientist.com/?articles.view/articleNo/38679/title/Pondering-Science-Publishing.
28. University of California, Santa Barbara, "Secrets of the 'Big Deal': The Pricing of Academic Journals and the Fleecing of University Libraries," https://www.library.ucsb.edu/sites/default/files/attachments/scholarly-communication/library-sponsored-programs-ucsb/Bergstrom-ucsblibrary.pdf; Theodore C. Bergstrom, Paul N. Courant, R. Preston McAfee, and Michael A. Williams, "Evaluating Big Deal Bundles," *PNAS* 111, 26 (June 16, 2014): 9425–9430.

29. Kathleen Robertson, "Mergers, Acquisitions, and Access: STM Publishing Today," *Library & Information Services in Astronomy,* https://www.eso.org/sci/libraries/lisa/lisa4/proceedings/Robertson.pdf.
30. Lutz Bornmann and Ruediger Mutz, "Growth Rates of Modern Science: A Bibliometric Analysis Based on the Number of Publications and Cited References," arXiv.1402.4578.
31. Rebecca Trager, "Chemical Sciences Literature Dominated by Five Publishing Houses," Chemistryworld, http://www.rsc.org/chemistryworld/2015/06/chemical-sciences-literature-dominated-big-five-publishing-houses.
32. Carolyn E. Lipscomb, "Mergers in the Publishing World," *Bulletin of the Medical Library Association* 89, 3 (July 2001): 307–308. Also see Jim Milliot, "The World's 52 Largest Book Publishers, 2016," *Publishers Weekly*, August 26, 2016, https://www.publishersweekly.com/../71268-the-world-s-52-largest-book-publishers-2016.html.
33. The Cost of Knowledge, http://www.thecostofknowledge.com; George Monbiot, "Scientific Publishing Is a Rip-Off. We Fund the Research—It Should Be Free," https://www.theguardian.com/commentisfree/2018/sep/13/scientific-publishing-rip-off-taxpayers-fund-research; George Monbiot, "Academic Publishers Make Murdock Look Like a Socialist," https://www.theguardian.com/commentisfree/2011/aug/29/academic-publishers-murdoch-socialist.
34. "San Francisco Declaration on Research Assessment," https://sfdora/read; Ralf Schimmer, "The Transformation of Scientific Journal Publishing: Open Access After the Berlin 12 Conference," *Information Services & Use* 37 (2017): 7–11. Also see Robert P. Holley, "Open Access: Current Overview and Future Prospects," *Library Trends* 67, 2 (Fall 2018): 214–240.
35. University of California Libraries, "Pathways to Open Access," Https://libraries.university.ofcalifornia.edu/groups/files/about/docs/UC-Libraries-Pathways%20to%20OA-report.pdf; Katherine Dunn, Hal Abelson, Chris Bourg, and Ellen Finnie, "Open Access at MIT and Beyond: A White Paper of the MIT Ad Hoc Task Force on Open Access to MIT's Research," DigitalCommons@University of Nebraska-Lincoln, http://digitalcommons.unl.edu/scholcom/92; Open Access Scholarly Publishers Association, "The International Community of Open Access Publishers," https://oaspa.org; Brian Satalino, "A Q & A With Jason Priem," https:/www.the-scientist.com/daily-news/open-access-on-the-state of-the rise-study-31125; "Large Scale Publishing Survey Reveals Global Trends in Open Access Publishing," https://blog.doaj.org/tag/academic-publishing; John Willinsky, "The Academic Library in the Face of Cooperative and Commercial Paths to Open Access," *Library Trends* 67,

2 (Fall 2018): 196–213; Initiative for Open Citations, "About," https://i4oc.org/#publishers.

36. Directory of Open Access Journals, "Latest News," https://doaj.org. Also see Heather Morrison, "Global OA APCs2010-2017: Major Trends," https://hal.archives-ouvertes.fr/hal-01816699.
37. "The Bill & Melinda Gates Foundation Open Access Policy," https://www.gatesfoundation.org/How-We-Work/General-Information/Open-Access-Policy. Science journals initially accepted the Gates Foundation mandate. Richard Van Noorden, "*Science* Journals Permit Open-Access Publishing for Gates Foundation Scholars," *Nature*, February 14, 2017, https://www.nature.com/news/science-journals-permit-open-access-publishing-for-gates-foundation-scholars-1.21486. The following year, *Science* journals revered their acceptance of the Gates Foundation's requirements. Richard Van Noorden, "Science Journals End Open-Access Trial With Gates Foundation," https://www.nature.com/articles/d41586-018-05729-2. Wellcome Trust, "Open Access Guidance," https://wellcome.ac.uk/funding/guidance/open-access.
38. Holly Else, "UK's Powerful Funding Body Takes Shape," https://www.nature.com/articles/d41586-018-05199-6.
39. "What Is cOAlition S?," https://www.coalition-s.org; Martin Enserink, "European Science Funders Ban Grantees From Publishing in Paywalled Journals," https://www.sciencemag.org/news/2018/09/european-science-funders-ban-grantees-publishingpaywalled-journals.
40. cOAlition S, "Making Full and Immediate Open Access a Reality," https://www.coalition-s.org/wp-content/uploads/271118_cOAlitionS_Guidance.pdf.
41. Ibid. For a list of the original 11 funders and supporters of Plan S, see https://www.coalition-s.org/funders-and-supporters. The Association of Research Libraries (ARL) supports Plan S; see Mary Lee Kennedy, "ARL Feedback on Plan Open Access Implementation Guidelines," https://mail.google.com/mail/u/1#inbox/FMfegxwBVWSgdlbghQzKhxnDvHMJxMpp; In 2019 the Canadian Association of Research Libraries (CARL) also supported Plan S; "Canadian Association of Research Libraries Submits Response to Plan S Implementation Guidance - 12 Feb 2019." Their response was as follows: "The Canadian Association of Research Libraries' members include Canada's twenty-nine largest university libraries as well as two national libraries. Enhancing research and higher education are at the heart of its mission. CARL develops the capacity to support this mission, promotes effective and sustainable scholarly communication, and public policy that enables broad access to scholarly information. Response from CARL to the Plan S Implementation Guidance: The Canadian Association of Research Libraries (CARL) is committed to

moving scholarly publishing towards maximum openness to advance innovation and sustainability of the system, while also ensuring that costs are controlled to maximize investment within the academy. CARL welcomes Plan S, a decisive commitment to achieve immediate open access for all publications stemming from research funded by its member organizations. Scholarly communication is global in nature, and Plan S will have a significant impact on scholarly publishing, both in the signatory countries and in other regions including Canada": http://www.carl-abrc.ca/wp-content/uploads/2019/02/CARL_Response_to_PlanS_2019.02.08.pdf. Jonathan V. Sweedler. "The Evolving World of Scientific Publications: From Unethical Behaviors to New Mandates From Funding Agencies," *Analytical Chemistry* 91 (February 5, 2019): 1673–1674.; Jenny Hoops and Sarah Hare, "Library Publisher Resources: Making Publishing Approachable, Sustainable, and Value-Driven," *C & RL News* (February 2019): 74–77; https://crin.acrl.org/index.php/crinews/article/viewFile/17580/19401.

42. Richard Van Noorden, "Wellcome and Gates Join Bold European-Access Plan," https://www.nature.com/articles/d41586-018-07300-5; Wellcome Trust, "Wellcome Is Updating Its Open Access Policy," https://wellcome.ac.uk/news/wellcome-updating-its-open-access-policy; Quirin Schiermeier, "China Backs Bold Plan to Tear Down Journal Paywalls," https://www.nature.com/articles/d41586-018-07659-5; Peter Suber, "Peter Suber, Thoughts on Plan S," http://tagteam.harvard.edu/hub_feeds/119/feed_items/2461573; Confederation of Open Access Repositories (COAR), "COAR's Feedback on the Guidance on the Implementation of Plan S," https://www.coar-repositories.org/news-media/coars-response-to-draft-implementation-requirements-in-plan-s; *Deutsche Forschungsgeminschaft*, "Information for Researchers No. 56/ 4 September 2018: DFG Statement on the Establishment of 'cOAlition S' to Support Open Access," http://www.dfg.de/en/research_funding/announcements_proposals/2018/info_wissenschaft_18_56/index.html; Ashley Yeager, "Open-Access Plan in Europe Bans Publishing in Paywalled Journals," https://www.the-scientist.com/news/-opinion/open-access-plan-in-europe-bans-publishing-in-paywalled-journals; Sicco de Knecht, "Editors of *Informetrics* Resign at Elsevier and Start New Journal," https://www.scienceguide.nl/2019/01/editorial-board-of-Informetrics-resigns-at-elsevier-and-start-new-journal; MIT News, "MIT Press to Co-Publish New Open-Access *Quantitative Science Studies* Journal," http://news.mit.edu/2019/new-quantitative-science-studies-journal-mit-press 0118. The journal will be copublished by MIT Press and the International Society for Scientometrics and Informetrics (ISSI); the journal will be "run for and by the scientometric community. The

initial editorial board will be fully constituted by the former editorial board of the Journal of Informetrics (JOI), an Elsevier-owned journal," https://www.mitpress/journals.org/journals/qss/editorial.

43. Charlotte J. Haug, "No Free Lunch—What Price Plan S for Scientific Publishing?," *New England Journal of Medicine*, February 16, 2019; https://www.nejm.org/doi/full/10.1056/NEJMms1900864. Also see Eanna Kelly, "Big Funders Back Plan for Instant Free Access to Journals, but Researchers Say It Is Risky for Science," https://sciencebusiness.net/framework-programmes/news/bi-funders-back-plan-instant-free-access-journals-researchers-say-it; Holly Else, "Radical Open-Access Plan Could Spell End to Journal Subscriptions," https://www.nature.com/articles/d41586-018-06178-7; Tania Rabesandratana, "Open-Access Plan Draws Online Protest," https://www.sciencemag.org/news/2018/11/open-access-plan-draws-online-protest; Brendan O'Malley, "Plan S for Open Access Is Far Too Risky, Say Researchers," http://www.universityworldnews.com/article.php?story=20181107234431569; Tania Rabesandratana, "Will the World Embrace Plan S, the Radical Proposal to Mandate Open Access to Science Papers?," https://www.sciencemag.org/news/2019/01/will-world-embrace-plan-s-radical-proposal-mandate-open-access-science-papers; Holly Else, "Architect of Bold European Open-Access Plan Heads to Washington to Garner U.S. Support," https://www.nature.com/articles/d41586-018-06936-7; Diana Kwon, "Plan S: The Ambitious Initiative to End Paywalls," https://www.the-scientist.com/news-opinion/plan-s-the-ambitious-initiative-to-end -the reign-of-paywalls-65231.
44. 17 U.S. C. §207. A complete copy of the Copyright Law of the United States, 17 U.S.C., is available at https://www.copyright.gov/title17. This publication contains the text of Title 17 of the United States Code, including all amendments enacted by Congress.
45. 17 U.S.C. §204.
46. 17 U.S.C. §106. "Exclusive rights in copyrighted works. Subject to sections 107 through 122, the owner of copyright under this title has the exclusive rights to do and to authorize any of the following: Copyright Law of the United States 17 Subject Matter and Scope of Copyright §106a (1) to reproduce the copyrighted work in copies or phonorecords; (2) to prepare derivative works based upon the copyrighted work; (3) to distribute copies or phonorecords of the copyrighted work to the public by sale or other transfer of ownership, or by rental, lease, or lending; (4) in the case of literary, musical, dramatic, and choreographic works, pantomimes, and motion pictures and other audiovisual works, to perform the copyrighted work publicly; (5) in the case of literary, musical, dramatic, and choreographic works, pantomimes, and pictorial, graphic,

or sculptural works, including the individual images of a motion picture or other audiovisual work, to display the copyrighted work publicly; and (6) in the case of sound recordings, to perform the copyrighted work publicly by means of a digital audio transmission."

47. U.S.C. §107. "Limitations on exclusive rights: Fair use notwithstanding the provisions of sections 106 and 106A, the fair use of a copyrighted work, including such use by reproduction in copies or phonorecords or by any other means specified by that section, for purposes such as criticism, comment, news reporting, teaching (including multiple copies for classroom use), scholarship, or research, is not an infringement of copyright. In determining whether the use made of a work in any particular case is a fair use the factors to be considered shall include—(1) the purpose and character of the use, including whether such use is of a commercial nature or is for nonprofit educational purposes; (2) the nature of the copyrighted work; (3) the amount and substantiality of the portion used in relation to the copyrighted work as a whole; and (4) the effect of the use upon the potential market for or value of the copyrighted work. The fact that a work is unpublished shall not itself bar a finding of fair use if such finding is made upon consideration of all the above factors."
48. Ibid.
49. 17 U.S.C. §201. "Ownership of copyright1 (a) Initial Ownership.—Copyright in a work protected under this title vests initially in the author or authors of the work. The authors of a joint work are co-owners of copyright in the work."
50. 17 U.S.C. §201(d) "Transfer of Ownership.—(1) The ownership of a copyright may be transferred in whole or in part by any means of conveyance or by operation of law, and may be bequeathed by will or pass as personal property by the applicable laws of intestate succession. (2) Any of the exclusive rights comprised in a copyright, including any subdivision of any of the rights specified by section 106, may be transferred as provided by clause (1) and owned separately. The owner of any exclusive right is entitled, to the extent of that right, to all of the protection and remedies accorded to the copyright owner by this title."
51. 17 U.S.C. §302. "Duration of copyright: Works created on or after January 1, 1978. (a) In General.—Copyright in a work created on or after January 1, 1978, subsists from its creation and, except as provided by the following subsections, endures for a term consisting of the life of the author and 70 years after the author's death. (b) Joint Works.—In the case of a joint work prepared by two or more authors who did not work for hire, the copyright endures for a term consisting of the life of the last surviving author and 70 years after such last surviving author's death."

52. Lariviere, Haustein, and Mongeon, "The Oligopoly of Academic Publishers in the Digital Era," *PloS One* (June 10, 2015). doi:10.1371/jpurnal.pone.0127502. The published literature on this topic is extensive. Some of the most important articles include: Harvard University Faculty Advisory Council, "Major Periodical Subscriptions Cannot Be Sustained," April 17, 2012, http://iites.harvard.edu/icb/icb.do?keywork=k77982&state=popup&topicid=icb.topic107; Jennifer Howard, "U. of California Tries Just Saying No to Rising Journal Costs," *Chronicle of Higher Education*, June 8, 2010, http://chronicle.com/article/U-of-California-Tries-Just/65823. See the Association of College and Research Libraries, http://www.ala.org/acrl.
53. Anon., "The Price of Information," *The Economist*, February 4, 2012: Elsevier "in 2010 it made £724 million ($1.16 billion) on profit on revenues of £2 billion, a margin of 36%": http://www.economist.com/node/21545974/print. Also see Laura McKenna, "The Convoluted Profits of Academic Publishing," *The Atlantic*, December 17, 2016, http://www.theatlantic.com/education/archive/2015/12/the-convoluted-profits-of-academic-puublishing; Noah Berlatsky, "Why Isn't Academic Research Free to Everyone?," *The Atlantic*, November 19, 2014, http://www.theatlantic.com/technology.archive/2014/11/why-isnt-academic-research-free-to-everyone; Richard Van Noorden, "Science Journals Permit Open-Access Publishing for Gates Foundation Scholars," *Nature*, February 14, 2017, http://www.nature.com/news/science-journals-permit-open-access-publishing-for-gates-foindation-scholars-1.21486.
54. Nature Index, "Ongoing Challenge," https://www.nature.com/articles/d41586-018-07688-0; Anita Makri, "Egypt and Pakistan Had the Highest Rise in Research Output in 2018," https://www.nature.com/articles/d41586-018-07841-9.
55. Valerie Spezi, Simon Wakeling, Stephen Pinfield, Claire Creaser, Jenny Fry, and Peter Willett, "Open-Access Mega-Journals: The Future of Scholarly Communication or Academic Dumping Ground? A Review," *Journal of Documentation* 73, 2 (2017): 263–283, https://doi.org/10.1108/JD-06-2016-0082.
56. Jeffrey Brainard, "Scientific Societies Worry Plan S Will Make Them Shutter Journals, Slash Services," https://www.sciencemag.org/news/2019/01/scientific-societies-worry-plan-s-will-make-them-shutter-journals-slash-services. Also see Melanie Schlosser, "Building Capacity for Academy-Owned Publishing Through the Library Publishing Coalition," *Library Trends* 67, 2 (Fall 2018): 359–375.
57. David Matthews, "Warning on 'Mirror Journals': European Commission Envoy Sees Attempt to Get Around Open-Access Requirement," https://www.insidehighered.com/news/2019/01/24/european-

commission-envoy-warns-about-mirror-journals-way-around-open-access?utm_source=Inside+Higher+Ed&utm_campaign=4fe094f8fe-DNU_2019_COPY_01&utm_medium=email&utm_term=0_1fcbc04421-4fe094f8fe-197325717&mc_cid=4fe094f8fe&mc_eid=82dc539218.

58. Springer Nature, file:///C:/Users/Al/Downloads/PRQU_Disclosure%20of%20interest%202011%20(5).pdf: "Conflict-of-Interest Disclosure Form. When an author or the institution of the author has a relationship, financial or otherwise, with individuals or organizations that could influence the author's work inappropriately, a conflict of interest may exist. Examples of potential conflicts of interest may include but are not limited to academic, personal, or political relationships; employment; consultancies or honoraria; and financial connections, such as stock ownership and funding. Although an author may not feel that there are conflicts, disclosure of relationships and interests that could be viewed by others as conflicts of interest affords a more transparent and prudent process. All authors and co-authors (if any) of papers submitted to [journal ABC] must complete this form and disclose any actual or potential conflict of interest. The journal may publish such disclosures. Please complete and return this form (one per author) and submit it/them together with your manuscript to the journal's Editorial Manager submission website. I have included a section, Conflict-of-Interest Statement, in the manuscript (applies even if there are no disclosures). I have no potential conflict of interest pertaining to this submission to [journal ABC]."
59. Anon., "Plan U: A Proposal to Achieve Universal Access to Scientific and Medical Research via Funder Preprint Mandates," http://planu.org.
60. Ibid.

[4]

THE PRODUCT AND PRICING OF SCHOLARLY BOOKS

INTRODUCTION: SCHOLARLY BOOK PUBLISHING HISTORY

Scholarly book publishing and printing has a long tradition, starting with Oxford University Press (1478) and Cambridge University Press (1584).[1] The American colonies, and later the United States, lived in the shadow of these two great presses.

Johns Hopkins University Press was created by Daniel Coit Gilman (the university's president) in 1878, and it is the first continually operated university press in the United States. Gilman believed that the university's mission was "to advance knowledge, and to diffuse it not merely among those who can attend the daily lectures—but far and wide."[2] Gilman's words struck a chord at other universities, and in the following decades, university presses were established at Chicago (1891), California and Columbia (both in 1893), Toronto (1901), Princeton (1905), Fordham (1907), Yale (1908), Washington (1909), Harvard (1913), New York (1916), Stanford (1917), and Illinois (1918).[3]

Oxford opened its US office in 1896; Cambridge waited until after the end of World War II (1949). "By 1919, fifty years after the establishment of the Cornell University Press, there were thirteen such presses in the United States and Canada. By 1939 . . . [there were] sixty-one presses."[4]

While many of these US presses today are quite large, with global operations, they were, in the late 19th century and the early years of the 20th century, "far from the professional operations of today. They often served as no more than job printers for universities, printing catalogues, unvetted faculty publications, or annual reports."[5] The early university presses grew slowly, often with part-time editorial personnel, and World War I and the Great Depression impacted publishing operations negatively.[6] Donald P. Bean's unpublished study "American Scholarly Publishing" indicated that, in the years after the end of World War I, university presses increased their publication of scholarly books.[7] Andre Fruge (formerly director of the University of California Press) wrote in *A Skeptic Among Scholars: August Fruge on University Publishing* that "in the nine years of 1934–1941, the [University of California] press brought out a little more than one hundred books, or about a dozen a year."[8]

The growth of university presses triggered interest in some type of informal organization to support their activities. John Tebbel, the historian of the US publishing industry, remarked that "in 1928 the [university press] group produced and circulated a joint catalog, Shelfward Ho, describing the books of thirteen presses."[9] While very informal annual meetings were held, the small university press group called itself the Association of American University Presses (AAUP; although AAUP had no legal standing), and the presses started to emerge from the clutches of the Great Depression, publishing more influential books. Even though almost every university press editor was trained primarily in the humanities, they began to adopt some semblance of a "competitive, entrepreneurial strategy."[10] Their progress did not go unnoticed within the confines of the scholarly trade book publishers; in the 1930s, trade book publishers published a number of scholarly tomes, many of which were acquired by academic libraries or adopted for classroom adoptions.[11] In 1936, the prominent trade book publisher "Farrar & Rinehart confronted the AAUP in June with a new division, it intended to call University Press Services, Inc."[12] This prompted the presses to create a "formal organization if only in self-defense against intrusions from commercial houses."[13]

COMPETITION TO UNIVERSITY PRESSES FROM COMMERCIAL PUBLISHERS

University press book publishing operations[14] face the same array of large, diversified, global commercial publishers, many with deep financial resources, as the journal sector (e.g., Elsevier, Kluwer, Sage, Wiley, Informa/Taylor & Francis, and Springer); however, there is one substantive difference. As in the 1930s and 1940s, trade book publishers are also active in the scholarly book sector, including Random House, Viking, and Penguin (all part of Penguin Random House); Free Press and Atheneum (both part of Simon & Schuster); Little, Brown, Basic Books, and Grand Central (all part of Hachette); St. Martin's Press, Henry Holt, and Farrar, Straus and Giroux (all part of Macmillan). In addition, there are major smaller presses active in the scholarly sector, including W. W. Norton.

In the years after the end of World War II, consolidation took place in both the commercial scholarly sphere and trade book publishing, creating companies that understood and took advantage of major strategic theories developed by Michael E. Porter, including creating competitive advantages, undertaking competitor analyses, and developing basic competitive positioning strategies (i.e., overall cost leadership, differentiation, focus, and middle of the road).[15]

By the 1980s, university presses faced the juggernaut of very successful commercial scholarly publishers and the large trade houses competing for major scholarly authors, offering advances, attractive royalties, and extensive US and foreign marketing operations. While Oxford, Cambridge, Harvard, Yale, Princeton, California, Chicago, and a few other large university presses could compete, within certain limits, with their commercial competitors, the vast majority of university presses could not. What these smaller university presses offered was the elusive notion of prestige associated with publishing with a university press and a close relationship with editors who loved books.[16] Peter Mayer, when he ran Penguin Books, once told this author that he originally hired editors who loved books, and then he realized that he had to hire editors who loved books that made money.

KEY SCHOLARLY PUBLISHING MARKET DRIVERS

Why does an individual or a library buy a scholarly book? What are the key market drivers in the scholarly book sector? Based on a number of discussions with scholarly book editors and publishers, the following six are very important market drivers for scholarly books.

The first market driver is the book's genre, perhaps American history. The book's topic (perhaps the administration of Franklin D. Roosevelt), category (political history), subcategory (political history of agriculture during the first New Deal), and sub-subcategory (political policies toward agriculture in Missouri during the first New Deal) are equally significant market drivers.

The second driver is the author's reputation in the academic discipline. Third, a critical market driver is whether the book is up to date, which is pivotal with scientific, technical, and medical (STM) books. Fourth, the reputation of the publisher, especially a university press, is an important reason to buy the book. Format is generally the fifth driver, especially for some readers and libraries. For example, is the book available as a hardcover or paperback book or an e-book? Is an individual chapter available for sale? Ironically, price is the sixth and least important market driver.

CHANNELS OF DISTRIBUTION

The channels of distribution for university presses and commercial scholarly publishers are rather similar, although monthly and annual sales data can vary significantly between university and commercial books when analyzing individual versus library purchases; the following percentages are rounded off and may not always equal 100%. Since basically 2010, channel distribution patterns for most, but clearly not all, scholarly book publishers are as follows. There is an intriguing similarity between online and physical bookstore sales. Traditionally, the largest channel of distribution has been to myriad wholesalers and jobbers, accounting for about 27% of all sales.[17] A recent 2019 report in *Library Acquisition Patterns* from Ithaka S + R stated that "the majority of print books published by university presses and acquired by academic libraries in this sample [of 124 academic libraries, a small but useful sample of major academic libraries] are sold and distributed through GOBI [i.e., Library Solutions, an academic book distributor]."[18] GOBI accounted for 68.7% of total print sales, reaching $17,723,709. Amazon was a distant second at 10.9% and $2,825,396. As for e-book sales, GOBI dominated this niche with 86.4% of all sales; Amazon did not make the list as one of the top 10 e-book distributors. Ebrary was ranked tenth with a 0.2% market share and $10,102 in sales.[19]

Slightly more than 26% of scholarly book sales were sold to various online retailers that may sell titles directly to readers and/or to libraries. Physical bookstores, including the national and regional chains; independent bookstores; and college bookstores accounted for about 26% of sales. The highly touted direct-to-consumer (D-2-C) channel and the e-book channels might develop into very important channel opportunities for presses, since profit margins are better with D-2-C and e-books, but so far both generate less than 15% of revenues.

The library market, while important, is small, with direct sales barely at the 2% level. However, an analysis of the datasets in *Library Acquisition Patterns* highlighted the actual size of this market. The two largest university presses with academic library sales were Oxford at $1,539,611 and Cambridge at $1,117,564. Yale ($264,620), Princeton ($222,056), and Harvard ($162,172) rounded out the top five.[20] E-book sales were rather small; Cambridge generated the largest amount at $217,904. Oxford ($127,127), Duke ($44,082), New York University ($40,853), and California ($39,557) were the top five presses in this category.[21] The remaining channels are also small, including special markets, remainders, and so forth.

Hardcover and paperback printed books each account for about 50% of sales revenues. As for print runs, about 50% of the presses order between 500 and 1,000 copies; the small presses often order fewer than 500 copies; and the large presses are often in the 1,000-plus print run category.

SIZE OF THE SCHOLARLY BOOK MARKET IN THE UNITED STATES: REVENUES AND NEW TITLE OUTPUT

The total amount of revenues generated by scholarly book publishers in the United States is the subject of serious debate. The Association of American Publishers (AAP) collects and aggregates annual scholarly book sales data from its members only for the years 2013–2017. Data before 2013, and back to 1998, was collected and aggregated by the Book Industry Study Group (BISG), which used annual data from the US Department of Commerce (Commerce). Commerce began a systemic data collection process in the last half of the 19th century; its annual publication *The Statistical Abstract of the United States* contains detailed datasets on a variety of topics, including books, from a broad swath of the entire United States, not just from members of a trade association.

While the data from *The Statistical Abstract of the United States* is exceptionally accurate and useful, their datasets pose a slight methodological problem because of the acceptance of the North American Industry Classification System (NAICS) by the United States, Mexico, and Canada in 1997 (and revised in 2002). The goal of NAICS was to harmonize business classification datasets issued by these three nations. NAICS replaced the old US Standard Industrial Classification (SIC) system. This meant that scholarly book industry data in *The Statistical Abstract of the United States*, following the NAICS guidelines, comingles sales revenues for university presses and commercial scholarly publishers into one category.

All things considered, one must accept the nationwide data collection in *The Statistical Abstract of the United States*. Table 4.1 lists the statistics from *The Statistical Abstract of the United States*.

Between 2001 and 2016, Yankee Book Peddler (one of the nation's most important book distributors) reported that university presses and commercial scholarly publishers released 971,035 new titles, literally an avalanche of new books.

University presses' total reached 178,532 during those years, averaging 11,158.25 annually during those 16 years. To put that tally into perspective, these presses released 30.24 titles every day of the year (including Saturdays and Sundays and four leap days), or 1.26 titles every hour of the day. Yet these totals pale in relation to the new title output of commercial scholarly publishers, which were a total of 792,503: 49,531.44 new titles annually, 134.23 every day of the year, and 5.59 every hour of every day in that 16-year period. Table 4.2 has the details.

To gain an overview of new title output, an analysis was done to highlight English literature books, which is generally the largest scholarly book category each year. Again, using the years 2001–2016 as a framework, university presses released 7,418 titles in this category. The total for commercial scholarly publishers was 30,743. Suggested retail prices (SRPs) for books varied annually, with university presses posting higher prices than the commercial publishers. Table 4.3 has the details. However, English literature was not the only category with a great deal of activity. Data from the university press association (formerly the Association of American University Presses, now called the Association of University Presses [AUP]) in 2019 revealed that 56 university presses had active lists in American literature, which is ironic since enrollment in literature classes in the United States sustained declines in recent years.[22] Table 4.4 has the details.

A similar pattern was evident in other book categories. Using physics as an example of new titles and SRPs in the STM sector between 2001 and 2016, university presses released 1,447 new titles,

Table 4.1 TOTAL SCHOLARLY BOOK PUBLISHING NET REVENUES (US MILLIONS OF DOLLARS), 2004–2016

Year	*Total Scholarly Book Revenues*
2001	$3,142
2002	$2,455
2003	$2,646
2004	$2,745
2005	$3,261
2006	$3,007
2007	$2,926
2008	$3,138
2009	$3,887
2010	$4,269
2011	$5,131
2012	$5,075
2013	$4,414
2014	$4,369
2016	$6,475
2016	$7,063

Source: *The Statistical Abstract of the United States 2001*, https://www.census.gov/library/publications/2002/compendia/statab/121ed.html;
The Statistical Abstract of the United States 2003, https://www.census.gov/library/publications/2003/compendia/statab/123ed.html;

Continued

Table 4.1 CONTINUED

The Statistical Abstract of the United States 2005, https://www2.census.gov/library/publications/2005/compendia/statab/125ed/tables/infocomm.pdf;
The Statistical Abstract of the United States 2006, https://www.census.gov/library/publications/2005/compendia/statab/125ed.html;
The Statistical Abstract of the United States 2008, https://www.census.gov/library/publications/2007/compendia/statab/127ed.html;
The Statistical Abstract of the United States 2009, https://www.census.gov/library/publications/2007/compendia/statab/127ed.html;
The Statistical Abstract of the United States 2010, https://www2.census.gov/library/publications/2010/compendia/statab/129ed/tables/infocomm.pdf;
The Statistical Abstract of the United States 2012, https://www.census.gov/library/publications/2011/compendia/statab/131ed.html;
The Statistical Abstract of the United States 2014, https://statabs-proquest-com.avoserv2.library.fordham.edu/ftv2/4c4e000001b556df.pdf;
The Statistical Abstract of the United States 2015, https://statabs-proquest-com.avoserv2.library.fordham.edu/ftv2/4c4e0000020f18f5.pdf;
The Statistical Abstract of the United States 2016, https://statabs-proquest-com.avoserv2.library.fordham.edu/ftv2/4c4e0000025ec4802016.pdf;
The Statistical Abstract of the United States 2017, https://statabs-proquest-com.avoserv2.library.fordham.edu/ftv2/4c4e000002b2595117.pdf;
The Statistical Abstract of the United States 2018, https://statabs-proquest-com.avoserv2.library.fordham.edu/ftv2/4c4e000003077f3c18.pdf, https://statabs-proquest-com.avoserv2.library.fordham.edu/ftv2/4c4e0000016a21d3.pdf;
The Statistical Abstract of the United States 2019, https://statabs-proquest-com.avoserv2.library.fordham.edu/ftv2/4c4e000002b2595119.pdf.

and commercial scholarly publishers' output reached 10,330. This meant that, during those years, scholarly book output topped 11,777, averaging 736.06 new titles annually, and 1.99 new titles every day of the week (including weekends, holidays, and leap-year days). Again, assuming no qualitative differences in physics books, the gap in SRPs was pronounced. In 2001, commercial scholarly publishers charged $35.74 more for their physics books than university presses; and by 2016, there was a $55.54 difference in SRPs. Table 4.5 has the details.

Table 4.2 NEW SCHOLARLY BOOK TITLE OUTPUT: UNIVERSITY PRESSES AND COMMERCIAL SCHOLARLY PUBLISHERS, 2001–2016

Year	*University Presses, Number of*		*Commercial Scholarly Publishers, Number of*		*Total Number of New Titles*
	New Books	*Average SRP*	*New Books*	*Average SRP*	
2001	10,130	$46.21	41,016	$60.99	51,146
2002	9,915	$46.69	43,554	$59.07	53,469
2003	11,104	$48.82	47,662	$61.08	58,766
2004	9,854	$51.64	44,981	$66.56	54,835
2005	9,812	$52.90	42,975	$69.13	52,787
2006	9,969	$54.68	47,124	$70.94	57,093
2007	10,781	$55.71	48,951	$71.15	59,732
2008	11,133	$57.79	52,116	$74.95	63,249
2009	12,070	$58.20	52,403	$78.67	64,473
2010	11,895	$59.86	51,802	$85.18	63,697
2011	12,064	$60.94	52,148	$86.17	64,212
2012	11,995	$62.63	53,047	$88.11	65,042
2013	11,710	$64.77	52,999	$92.68	64,709
2014	11,791	$72.96	54,831	$93.84	66,622
2015	12,056	$64.28	52,540	$96.74	64,596
2016	12,253	$65.44	54,354	$97.51	66,607
Total	178,532	—	792,503	—	971,035

N.B. Average SRP is the average suggested retail price, which excludes any discounts.

Source: Yankee Book Peddler.

Table 4.3 NEW TITLE OUTPUT OF ENGLISH LITERATURE BOOKS, 2001–2016

Year	*University Presses*		*Commercial Scholarly Presses*		*Total New Books*
	New Books	*Average SRP*	*New Books*	*Average SRP*	
2001	505	$43.12	1,597	$32.51	2,102
2002	448	$41.06	1,658	$30.70	2,106
2003	515	$42.85	1,748	$33.59	2,263
2004	450	$50.19	1,370	$36.54	1,820
2005	412	$51.39	1,338	$37.69	1,750
2006	376	$55.41	1,827	$35.35	2,203
2007	435	$66.20	2,090	$38.68	2,525
2008	459	$60.76	2,030	$39.98	2,489
2009	619	$46.76	2,086	$46.42	2,705
2010	484	$56.89	2,255	$38.02	2,739
2011	459	$64.37	1,959	$42.30	2,418
2012	472	$66.29	2,112	$40.91	2,584
2013	415	$65.76	1,984	$39.80	2,399
2014	472	$65.90	2,199	$42.19	2,671
2015	460	$65.14	2,226	$34.82	2,686
2016	437	$67.99	2,264	$37.53	2,701
Total	7,418	—	30,743	—	38,161

Source: Yankee Book Peddler.

Table 4.4 UNIVERSITY PRESSES PUBLISHING TITLES IN AMERICAN LITERATURE, 2019

Abilene/Chr.	Delaware	McGill/Queen's	Northwestern	Temple
Akron	Duke	Manchester	Notre Dame	Tennessee
Alabama	Florida	U. Mass.	Ohio Univ.	Texas
Baylor	Fordham	Mercer	Ohio State	Texas/Chr.
Beacon	Gallaudet	Michigan	Oxford	Texas Tech
California	Georgia	Mich. State	Penn State	Tokyo
Cambridge	Harvard	Minnesota	Princeton	Vanderbilt
CMU	Illinois	Mississippi	Rutgers	Wisconsin
Catholic	Iowa	Missouri	So. Carolina	
Chicago	Kent State	MLA	So. Illinois	
Columbia	Liverpool	New England	Stanford	
Cornell	Louisiana	No. Carolina	Syracuse	

N.B. "Chr." is the abbreviation for Christian for Abilene Christian and Texas Christian. "CMU" is Carnegie Mellon University. "MLA" is the Modern Language Association.

Source: Association of University Presses, http://www.aaup.net.

While humanities and the social sciences (HSS) generally generate the most interest, STM was of concern to academics and researchers because of the high prices for these titles.[23]

Collectively, this meant that the United States faced a barrage of 60,689.69 new books every year, 164.47 new books every day, and 6.85 new books every hour of every day. It is hard to understand how the US market, even when evaluating the exportation of scholarly books to other nations, can absorb this outpouring of books, which might

Table 4.5 NEW TITLE OUTPUT OF PHYSICS BOOKS, 2001–2016

Year	*University Presses*		*Commercial Scholarly Presses*		*Total New Books*
	New Books	*Average SRP*	*New Books*	*Average SRP*	
2001	104	$68.96	576	$104.70	680
2002	85	$80.49	554	$107.80	639
2003	86	$73.57	630	$104.72	716
2004	88	$79.26	606	$122.52	694
2006	104	$80.23	527	$125.31	631
2006	76	$79.71	626	$120.41	702
2007	119	$76.92	695	$117.29	814
2008	94	$83.14	524	$120.05	618
2009	101	$81.25	651	$122.65	752
2010	131	$74.95	635	$133.97	766
2011	114	$79.36	678	$130.68	792
2012	132	$78.99	724	$130.54	856
2013	101	$80.80	723	$136.34	824
2014	89	$76.33	753	$127.13	842
2015	121	$78.47	699	$135.63	820
2016	106	$76.47	729	$132.01	835
Total	1,447	—	10,330	—	11,777

Source: Yankee Book Peddler.

explain the hefty return rates for scholarly books. Table 4.6 has the details.

While these statistics are rather unsettling, what is more perplexing is the fact that the commercial publishers, because of their size and access to financial markets, have scale, something that has eluded most university presses, and 16 years of data revealed that commercial publishers charged a higher suggested retail price than university presses. While the gap in SRPs in 2001 was only $14.48 (the university press SRP was $46.21, commercial publisher SRP $60.99), by 2016 the difference was $32.07 (university press SRP $65.44, commercial publisher SRP $97.51). Table 4.3 has the details.

The author interviewed a number of individuals at university presses and commercial publishing houses, and no qualitative difference was ever discovered between books published by university presses and their commercial brethren. So, the gap in SRPs seems quite odd even if one factors in university press revenue streams from endowments, subventions, and so forth. Clearly, university presses need to reevaluate their pricing strategies.

HOW MUCH DOES IT COST TO PUBLISH A BOOK?

University presses had to become more "business-like" because of intense competition from commercial scholarly publishers, sharp increases in expenses, and, at a number of universities, questions about subsidies and the importance of the press in the university's mission. Over the years, the AUP attempted to provide practical advice, at seminars and at the annual meeting, for press directors, editors, and either business managers employed at a press or university budget officials who supplied financial advice to a press.

One early attempt to assist presses took place in 1977 at the AAUP annual meeting. Detailed information about calculating realistic

Table 4.6 SCHOLARLY BOOK PUBLISHER RETURN RATES, 2001–2016

Year	*University Presses*		*Commercial Scholarly Publishers*
	Hardcover	*Paperback*	
2001	20.2%	24.6%	19.8%
2002	25.2%	25.3%	19.0%
2003	19.5%	23.8%	21.4%
2004	15.4%	14.0%	19.6%
2005	16.3%	13.4%	19.1%
2006	16.3%	22.1%	17.9%
2007	17.6%	22.2%	17.9%
2008	21.1%	25.3%	18.3%
2009	20.5%	23.5%	18.6%
2010	19.0%	22.5%	17.4%
2011	19.4%	21.6%	17.8%
2012	20.9%	22.6%	16.8%
2013	20.5%	21.4%	15.7%
2014	22.1%	21.4%	13.7%
2015	20.8%	19.92%	12.8%
2016	21.1%	19.31%	15.65%

N.B. All numbers rounded off and may not always equal 100%.

Source: Association of American Publishers.

profit and loss statements was presented as "the log of the 'manuscript project' of the Association of American University Presses, in which five presses put one manuscript through their various publishing procedures from initial appraisal to production planning and the working out of a marketing program."[24]

Five presses volunteered in 1977 to prepare detailed editorial, production, financial, and marketing data for a print run of 7,500 copies for the same book. Clearly, the presses (Chicago, MIT, North Carolina, Texas, and Toronto) dealt with different printers, used "similar" trim cutoffs and paper, and had different organizational expenses. While the cost estimates and results were discussed in 1977, interest in helping presses prompted in 1994 the publication of all of the 1977 materials in *One Book/Five Ways: The Publishing Procedures of Five University Presses* by the University of Chicago Press. This book provides an intriguing view of how these scholarly publishers viewed the existing market for scholarly books (which could absorb a 7,500 print run) and estimated costs for a title that they assumed would have, in several instances, substantial sell-through rates.

The total cost estimates for the same book were as follows: Chicago, $11,219; MIT, $9,399; North Carolina, $10,019; Texas, $13,275; and Toronto $19,051. *One Book/Five Ways: The Publishing Procedures of Five University Presses* did not stipulate if Toronto's cost estimates were in US or Canadian dollars. Not every press indicated sell-through rates, but Chicago assumed a 7,250 sell-through (96.67%), and MIT's three-year 100% rate was interesting.[25]

A more recent analysis was published in 2016. Nancy Maron, Kimberly Schmelzinger, Christine Mulhern, and Daniel Rossman analyzed datasets from 20 university presses in "The Costs of Publishing Monographs: Toward a Transparent Methodology" to ascertain costs for scholarly books. Again, this was another small sample, but their results revealed that titles in the art and architecture field had the highest average costs at $39,654.71, with science just behind at $36,603.63. The least expensive was anthropology at $21,696.95, with history ($28,996.74), the humanities ($28,598.06), and area studies ($28,373.74) clustered in the center of the list.[26] Table 4.7 has the details.

THE SCHOLARLY BOOK VALUE CHAIN AND BOOK PROPOSAL

The value chain in the scholarly book sector is more complex than what is typically found in the scholarly journal industry. An author

Table 4.7 AVERAGE BASIC COST PER TITLE BY DISCIPLINE

Academic Subject Area	*Average Cost per Title*
American Studies	$29,354.65
Anthropology	$21,696.95
Art/Architecture	$39,654.71
Archaeology	$30,528.80
Area Studies	$28,373.74
Arts/Film	$31,317.31
History	$28,996.74
Humanities	$28,598.06
Religion	$19,427.28
Science	$36,603.63
Social Science	$26,819.29

N.B. Based on data supplied by 20 university presses.

Source: Nancy Maron, Kimberly Schmelzinger Christine Mulhern, and Daniel Rossman, "The Costs of Publishing Monographs: Toward a Transparent Methodology."

starts with an idea for a business history book, perhaps a business history of the US radio industry since 1920. The author reads the published literature, visits some archives (perhaps the New York Public Library or the Library of Congress), and interviews some industry executives. The author then faces a hypothetical "fork in the road" since there are two very different strategies for the author to consider.

In the first option, the author could first spend months, if not years, writing the book and then sending the manuscript (known as an ms. in the publishing world) to an editor at a scholarly publisher (perhaps Princeton University Press). This process is called a "cold" or an "over the transom" submission. The editor could review the proposal and either reject it (a bench review) or ask the author to make a series of additions. The revision would be sent to the editor, who would evaluate it and, if he or she thought the ms. had merit, send the ms. out for peer review. The reviewers could recommend that the ms. be accepted "as is," recommend that the author consider a series of additions and deletions, or recommend that the press reject the ms. The editor will review the reviewer's comments and accept the ms. "as is," ask the author to make the changes and resubmit the ms., or reject the ms.

The author has a second option. The author could prepare a detailed book proposal and send it to the editor at Princeton. The Princeton editor would repeat the steps listed previously for a completed ms., and the author could possibly receive a book contract before writing one sentence of a completed ms.

The first option could work, and the author could receive a contract, or the editor could reject the ms. This means the author will have to submit the ms. to one or more editors, and the end result could be a completed ms. that sits on a shelf and is never published. The second option allows the author to "hedge" his or her bets, that is, to find out if a book contract was tendered before spending months or years working on the ms. In essence, the author could write a complete ms. on "spec" (i.e., speculate that the end result will be positive) or write a book proposal, which could minimize months or years of unsuccessful work on an ms.

A "typical" book proposal contains the following. The first part includes a proposed book title and a detailed description of the book's thesis. This information provides an anchor for the book, and it informs an editor about the book's substantive ideas regarding the book's time period (in this case 1920–2020), major events, the impact of disruptive technologies, and a list of important managerial, marketing, financial, and copyright issues.

The second part of the proposal is the book's synopsis, which includes material regarding the focus of the book (and what book categories are included and excluded), the projected length of the ms. (120,000 words), available statistical data (which is very important for a business historical work), and the important proposed table of contents (TOC in book publishing). In addition, an editor wants to know why there is a need for this book, and the proposal must address this issue to convince the editor to support this proposal among all of the ones evaluated at the editorial meeting at Princeton.

The third key element is the target market for this book. Again, editors need to know if it warrants the money it will cost to publish a business history book. The fourth element centers on what are the competing books in this sector, again another important possible economic consideration for an editor and editorial board members.

If all goes well, with either the first (the "spec" ms.) or second option (the book proposal), a book contract will be sent to the author. Then the author and the editor want to make sure a "publishable" ms. is submitted, so the ms. goes through the typical value chain: editorial review, sales and marketing, production, print, and distribution to the important retail bookstores as well as online operations.

THE TYPICAL BOOK CONTRACT

A book contract is a complex document since it states and addresses substantive issues regarding word count, delivery dates, advances, royalties, and so forth. While every book contract is different, the following is a typical contract for a scholarly book. This is not a contract from Oxford University Press.

MEMORANDUM OF AGREEMENT

Made this 1st day of AAA year BBB:

between [AUTHOR CCC (hereinafter called "the Author," which expression shall where the context admits include the Author's executors administrators and assigns)] of the one part and **[PUBLISHER DDD]** (hereinafter called "the Publisher," which expression shall where the context admits include the Publisher's executors, and assigns or successors in business as the case may be)] of the other part.

WHEREBY it is mutually agreed between the parties hereto as follows:

§1. GRANT AND DELIVERY

The Author hereby grants the Publisher the sole and exclusive right and license to produce and publish in all languages, editions, in both printed and electronic form, in whole or in part, and in any media now known or later developed, throughout the world for the legal term of copyright a Work now entitled: [BOOK TITLE EEE].

§2. DELIVERY AND ACCEPTANCE

2.1 The Author undertakes to deliver to the Publisher by 1 July FFF the final and complete Work consisting of not more than 120,000 words to include figures, illustrations, tables, notes, and references (allowing 500 words for each figure or illustration and 300 words for each table included) as a digital copy in MS Word format. The Author's Word files will be prepared in accordance with the instructions provided by the Publisher. Any diagrams, charts, illustrations, and maps in a form suitable for reproduction by the Publisher. Preliminary pages and end matter including a table of contents, endnotes, and bibliography. Should the Author neglect to deliver the typescript by the prescribed date, the Publisher may either extend the time in writing or terminate this Agreement, whereby the Author will be obliged to return any monies which may have been advanced to him under this Agreement.

2.2 If the Author submits a manuscript which, in the opinion of the Publisher, does not meet the standard envisaged at the date of this Agreement, in both form and content, the Publisher may, if he thinks fit, decline to publish the Work in which case this Agreement shall be terminated, and the Author will be obliged to return any monies which may have been advanced to him under this Agreement, or as a condition of acceptance of the Work the Publisher shall require the Author to make amendments to the Work to ensure that it does meet the standard envisaged. The Publisher reserves the right to alter or insist that the Author alters the text of the Work in such a way as may appear to the Publisher appropriate for the purpose of removing or amending any passage which on the advice of the Publisher's legal advisers may be considered objectionable or likely to be actionable at law without affecting the Author's liability under Clause 3 hereof in respect of any passage not so removed or amended. In the event that the final and complete typescript of the Work is longer than specified in Clause 2, the Publisher is free either to reduce the royalties specified in §7 or to require that the Author reduce the length of the text accordingly.

2.3 The Author shall not be entitled to make any substantive changes or revisions to the Work once it is in the course of production, save for changes indicated by the copy-editor, or correcting errors that may have been introduced during the typesetting stage. The index may be supplied by the Author within 21 days of receipt of the final page proofs. If the Author is unable to supply the index, it shall be supplied by the Publisher and the cost shall be deducted from any sum which may become payable to the Author under the terms of this Agreement.

2.4 The Author is responsible for obtaining from the owners of any material in the Work, of which the copyright is not his own, written permission for the use of such material in all forms, including printed and electronic. The written record of all transactions and agreements regarding copyright permissions will be maintained in good order by the Author and transmitted, in complete form, to the Publisher upon his request. Any previously published material included in the book shall be fully referenced. This includes material that has been previously published by the Author.

2.5 The Author undertakes to read and check proofs of the Work and to return them to the Publisher within 14 days of their receipt and to bear the amount, if any, by which the costs of the Author's alterations, other than typesetter's errors, exceeds 10% of the cost of composition. When requested to do so, the Author will supply a description of the Work of between 100 and 300 words at any time prior to publication and for the purpose of promotion and advertisement.

2.6 The Publisher shall not be responsible for any accidental loss or damage to the editorial matter, including illustrations and other materials, by fire or otherwise, while it is in his custody, or in the course of production.

§3. *AUTHOR'S WARRANTY*

The Author hereby warrants to the Publisher that: the Author is the sole legal owner of the copyright in the Work, and has the right and power to make this Agreement; the Work is an original Work and will in no way whatsoever give rise to a violation of any existing copyright or a breach of any existing agreement; the Work contains nothing defamatory or libelous and all statements contained therein purporting to be facts are true. The Author will indemnify the Publisher against any loss, injury, or damage (including any legal costs or expenses and any compensation costs and disbursements paid by the Publisher on the advice of the Publisher's legal advisers to compromise or settle any claim) arising out of any breach or alleged breach of the foregoing warranties. The foregoing warranties and indemnity shall survive the termination of this Agreement.

§4. PUBLICATION

4.1 Save as hereby otherwise provided, the Publisher shall, unless prevented by war, strikes, lock-outs, or other circumstances beyond his control, produce, publish, and advertise the Work at his own risk and expense. The Publisher shall have entire control of the publication and the paper, printing, binding, jacket, and embellishments; the style and time of production; the manner and extent of advertisement; the number and distribution of free copies for the Press or otherwise; and the price and terms of sale of the first or any subsequent edition, shall be in his sole discretion. The Publisher agrees to consult with the Author over the content of the book cover.

§5. COPYRIGHT AND INFRINGEMENT

5.1 The Publisher, upon first publication of the Work, agrees duly to register the copyright in the Work in the name of the Author and to imprint the copyright notice required by law in each copy of the Work. The Author agrees to furnish the Publisher promptly with any authorization or documentation necessary to carry out these provisions. In the event that the copyright is infringed, the parties may agree jointly to bring suit, and in such event the expenses and recovery shall be divided equally between the parties. In the event that only one of the parties shall bring suit he shall do so at his own expense and be entitled to the entire recovery; and the other party agrees to cooperate, but without expense to him.

5.2 The Author of this Work has asserted his right to be identified as the author in accordance with GGG sections of HHH; and the Publisher recognizes his right to be identified as the author to be described in the Work and all publicity related to it as the author of the Work.

§6. CONFLICTING WORKS

6.1 While the Work is in course of preparation or in current publication, the Author shall be entitled to use material written or compiled by him for the purposes of the Work in articles submitted to learned or professional journals, in papers presented at professional conferences, and for the Author's professional purposes generally, provided that the Author so advises the Publisher in advance and makes appropriate acknowledgment to the Work and the Publisher; but the Author shall not without the written consent of the Publisher write or edit, jointly or severally, any Work which might reasonably be considered by the Publisher to compete with or prejudice sales of the Work or the exploitation of any of the rights granted to the Publisher under this Agreement.

§7. PAYMENTS

7.1 The Publisher agrees to remit to the Author the following royalties or fees in respect of sales of the Work:

7.2 On the net amount of all copies sold of any hardback edition of the Work: 10% of the Publisher's net receipts after 500 copies are sold. On the net amount of all copies sold of any paperback edition of the Work: 5% of the Publisher's net receipts after 500 copies are sold; 10% on the next 1,000 copies; and 12.5% thereafter. Should the Publisher publish the Work (or any part thereof), or any adaptation or abridgement of the Work, or license the Work in electronic form, by exercising their electronic publishing rights, the Publisher shall pay to the Author a royalty based on the net sum received by the Publisher in respect of sales of the Work in whole or in part in electronic form. On the net amount of all sales of the Work in electronic form: 5% of the Publisher's net receipts on the first $7,500.00 of net receipts, and 10% thereafter. In consideration of the payment to the Author of the applicable percentages of the Publisher's receipts listed below, the Author grants to the Publisher the sole and exclusive right during the period of this Agreement to exercise and/or license others to exercise all of the Subsidiary Rights hereinafter following, the Author and the Publisher shall each receive 50% of any revenues from: anthology and quotation rights; book clubs; reprints in book forms; and translations.

§8. FREE COPIES

No royalties shall be paid in respect of the following:

8.1 Copies of the Work presented to the Author or to others or to the Press or deposited for copyright purposes, or presented as trade samples. Copies of the Work destroyed by fire, water, enemy action, or in transit, or otherwise. Copies of the Work sold at or below the costs of production or sold to the Author, or to a third party at his direction, at a special price agreed with the Publisher.

§9. AUTHOR'S COPIES

9.1 The Author shall be entitled to receive on publication 6 gratuitous copies of the first edition of the Work. The Author shall also be entitled to receive 6 gratuitous copies of any subsequent paperback edition of the Work and 1 copy of any subsequent reprinted edition of the Work. The Author shall have the right to purchase his own Work and other titles on the Publisher's list for personal use but not for resale with a 50% discount off the published price, provided that payment is made with order. There will be a separate handling charge to include the cost of postage and packing.

§10. ACCOUNTING AND TAX

10.1 The Publisher shall render the account of the said Work annually as at June 30th, and all monies due to the Author shall be paid to the Author within three months of the said accounting date, provided, however, that no account need be submitted unless specially demanded nor payment made in respect of each year in which the sum due is less than $50.00, in which case the amount will be carried forward to the next accounting date.

10.2 The Publisher may deduct from any amount due to the Author under this Agreement, any sum that the Publisher is or may be under statutory obligation to deduct in respect of any tax, duty, or other similar levy. All sums due to the Author hereunder are exclusive of JJJ, which shall, where applicable, be paid in addition at the rate in force at the time of payment. Should the Author neglect to provide details of the Author's LLL registration number, the Publisher shall not pay JJJ on any sums due to the Author under this Agreement.

§11. REMAINDER

If the Work ceases to have a remunerative sale, the Publisher shall be entitled to sell any surplus stock as a remainder at the best price such remainder stock will fetch.

§12. OUT OF PRINT

12.1 If the Work shall become out of print and not be available in any edition, including electronic editions, issued by the Publisher or authorized by him, the Author may give nine months' notice in writing to the Publisher to reissue or reprint the Work. In the event of the Publisher's failure to comply with such notice other than through circumstances beyond his control all of the Publisher's rights in the Work shall upon expiration of the said notice terminate without prejudice to all rights of the Publisher or any third party in respect of any Agreement properly entered into by the Publisher hereunder with any such party provided that the Author shall refund to the Publisher any advance payment as yet unearned made in accordance with Clause 7 hereof. The Author's requirement that the Work be reprinted shall be regarded as satisfied if at the time of the Author's giving notice the Publisher has subleased rights for an edition scheduled for publication within 12 months of such notice being given.

§13. TERMINATION

If the Publisher at any time by himself or anyone acting on his behalf willfully fails to fulfill or comply with any of the conditions accepted by him in this Agreement within one month after written notification from the Author of such failure, or should the Publisher go into liquidation, other than voluntary liquidation for purposes of reconstruction, this Agreement shall thereupon terminate and the Author shall be free to license any other person to print and publish the editorial matter, notwithstanding anything to the contrary contained or implied in any part of this Agreement but without prejudice to all rights of the Publisher and any third party in respect of any Agreement properly entered into by the Publisher hereunder with any such party.

§14. LAW AND ARBITRATION
This Agreement is governed by the law of [county] MMM.

SIGNATURE OF CONTRACT

Please insert your date of birth and nationality. This information is required by the Library of Congress, and this is essential to the marketing of your book in the US.

DATE OF BIRTH ____________ NATIONALITY ______________________
SIGNED BY [AUTHOR] ________ SIGNED BY THE PUBLISHER _________
DATE__________________________ DATE ___________________________

ANALYSIS OF THE CONTRACT

While every book contract is different, they all contain basic terms and conditions, often called "boilerplate" since they are attached to the contract.

The first paragraph stipulated the date the contract was made between the publisher and the author, and that the following sections of the contract were "mutually agreed" to by the author and publisher.

Section 1 conveys the copyright to the publisher, thereby granting the publisher "sole and exclusive rights" to publish the book and handle all subrights and foreign rights. While Title 17 U.S.C. is not mentioned, the author is bound by 17 U.S.C., which gives the publisher the copyright for as long as the author is alive and 70 years after the death of the author. The book title is listed. While the author creates the book title, some publishers often make recommendations to "modify" the title for marketing reasons; most authors comply with a "reasonable" marketing recommendation.

Section 2 contains a great deal of relevant information that requires the author's close attention, including a pivotal delivery date of the manuscript in Microsoft Word (the publisher provides a style manual) and a maximum word count including "figures, illustrations, tables, notes, and references" suitable for reproduction. The publisher's word count for these items should be followed carefully; however, an early request for an extension is almost always allowed. The author can request a different style manual; for example, the *Chicago Manual of Style* is generally accepted for books in the humanities.[27] Section 2 also addresses the "publishability" of the manuscript. If the publisher ascertains the manuscript is not "publishable," the publisher can terminate the contract and request the return of any advance. The publisher also has the right to request the author to revise any section(s) of the manuscript and/or rewrite any section(s) that could be viewed as libelous. If the manuscript's word count exceeds the maximum in this section, the publisher can request that the author either reduce the word count or have the royalty reduced.

After the manuscript is submitted and goes into production, the author is limited to identifying printer errors (know as PEs) in the manuscript. Author's alterations (known as AAs) might be allowed, although some publishers will charge a fee for AAs beyond a certain limit.

The author has the option of preparing the book's index (at best a tedious project) or allowing the publisher to hire a professional indexer, with the indexer's costs subtracted from any royalty payment. The author must obtain any written permissions for material included in the manuscript. The author must read the page proofs, identifying any PEs, and prepare a brief abstract of the book for various purposes, including metadata identification and marketing of the book in catalogs, the publisher's online website, and publisher-prepared documents (known as "tip sheets" in the industry) used by sales representatives calling on book buyers at book chains, independent bookstores, and online bookselling sites. The publisher will not be responsible for any damage of the manuscript while it is in the author's possession and/or in production.

Section 3 is the traditional "author holds harmless" statement, which is found in almost every (or in every) book contract, that stipulates that the author will "hold harmless" the publisher. It states that the author is the author of the manuscript (i.e., possible defamation and/or libelous and/or copyright infringement issues under Title 17 U.S.C.), has the legal right to convey the manuscript to the publisher (again potential copyright infringement issues), and will indemnify the publisher for any expenditures related to any lawsuit regarding the manuscript, and that the ms. contains nothing that could be viewed as being defamatory and/or libelous.

However, in a legal proceeding, a plaintiff will sue for "damages," which can be substantial and have to be proven in a trial. Since most authors do not have vast financial resources, a plaintiff will also name the publisher in any legal suit since the publisher probably has various business insurance policies (and possibly a policy regarding defamation and/or libel); this means that the publisher has "deep pockets" (i.e., large financial resources) or at least "deeper pockets" than the author. This enables the plaintiff to maintain, possibly, that the publisher and/or the publisher's employees (e.g., editors) did not follow any "due diligence" in inspecting the manuscript before it was published and, accordingly, the publisher was also guilty of defamation and/or libel and/or copyright infringement. Since legal proceedings can be very expensive (some lawyers can charge $1,000 or more per hour, and some "publishing industry experts" hired by the author and/or the publisher can charge $600 or more per hour), many of these lawsuits are settled out of court to minimize expenditures and bad publicity for the author, the publisher, or, in many instances, the large corporation that owns the publisher.

Section 4 contains detailed terms that come as a surprise to many first-time authors. This means that, once the author and publisher sign the contract, the publisher, and not the author, owns the manuscript and has "complete" control over the manuscript in the production cycle as well as advertising and promotions. Some authors request that the book's paper stock be of a certain color and weight; others recommend certain cover illustrations (sometimes designed by the author) or the color of the print on the cover. While an author can make these requests, and the contract states that "the publisher agrees to consult with the author over the content of the book cover," the publisher controls all of these issues; the author's requests might be accepted or rejected.

Section 5 addresses Title 17 U.S.C., which has detailed information about the copyright process and infringement issues. A few experienced authors read through Title 17 U.S.C. (which is rather detailed and quite long). Other authors consult the useful and readable copyright documents from the US Copyright Office, known as "Circulars." For example, there are freely available "Circulars" on "Copyright Basics," "Renewal of Copyright," "Duration of Copyright," and "How to Investigate the Copyright Status of a Work."[28]

Section 6 allows the author to use content from the book in various scholarly activities, including journals and presentations, as long as the author "advises the publisher in advance." Another key provision addresses the concept of "noncompeting" works; in this matter, the author is prohibited from writing another book that competes "with or prejudices sales of the work" listed in the contract.

Section 7 covers issues of concern to any author, payments related to the book. The author will receive 10% of net sales of the hardcover version of the book (i.e., gross sales minus returns equals net sales) after 500 net sales are posted. Paperback versions of the book could be issued simultaneously with the publication of the hardcover version (known as a "hard and soft" release). In some instances, paperbacks are released sometime after the hardcover is released. A delay could be advantageous to the publisher since a "hard and soft" release could encourage academic libraries to purchase the paperback, with a lower SRP than the hardcover's SRP, and send the paperback to a bindery to have a "hard cover" attached. This procedure can negatively impact hardcover sales. Paperback sales have a lower royalty rate for the first 1,000 sold, and very few scholarly books reach that level. The publisher offers a "step" royalty system beyond 1,000 sales: 10% on sales between 1,001 and 1,999, and 12.5% on sales +2,000. In addition, royalty rates are listed for adaptations, abridgements, and electronic rights. Again, since the publisher has "sole and exclusive rights" under the contract, a step system is stipulated regarding sales on the first $7,500.00 (5%), and 10% on revenues above that amount. Sales for anthologies, quotation rights, book clubs, reprints, and translations (and translations have great potential in the global rights marketplace) are shared on a 50%/50% basis between the publisher and the author.

Section 8 states that no royalties will be paid on free copies provided by the publisher or copies "sold at or below the costs of production." This last reference is the sale of books deemed "out of print" by the publisher and sold as "remainders" into various channels, including sales of a title in boxes or on skids at the Chicago International Remainder & Overstock Expo (known as CIROBE). CIROBE organizes remainder operations in Chicago every fall, and also has a presence at Book Expo (generally in New York City in late May or early June).[29]

Section 9 states that the publisher will provide the author with six free copies of any hardcover book and six frees copies for any paperback version. Since many authors want to give a copy to family members, associates, friends, etc., the author can purchase addition copies at a 50% discount off the SRP.

Section 10 outlines the publisher's responsibilities regarding notifying the author, in this instance annually, of all sales and royalties earned by the author. However, any royalty earned annually below $50.00 will be carried forward until the next payment period. The publisher must account for and deduct any taxes the author might owe of the earned royalty.

Section 11 outlines the publisher's remainder option. Section 12 again asserts the authority of the publisher to declare a book "out of print." Section 13 lists in some detail the author's right to terminate the contract if any of the specified conditions occur (including failure of the publisher to perform its obligations under the contract or the liquidation of the publisher). Section 14 describes relevant legal and arbitration options available to the author and the publisher. In the United States, arbitration issues are often handled by the American Arbitration Association.[30]

The last section requires both parties to sign and date the contract. Under cataloguing requirements of the Library of Congress, the author is required to complete the nationality portion of the signature page.

SCHOLARLY HARDCOVER BOOK PROFIT AND LOSS STATEMENT

The basic elements of a profit and loss (P&L) statement for a printed hardcover scholarly book are "essentially" the same at a university press and a commercial scholarly publisher since both want to estimate total costs and contributions to the publishing operation. There can be differences, and in some instances significant differences, in how a P&L statement is evaluated and used; cost differences in printing, paper, and binding (PPB) expenditures and overhead; and differences in what is actually included in a P&L statement. "Books," "copies," "titles," and "units" can be used interchangeably in the scholarly publishing sector.

However, a book P&L statement is a complex estimated sales and costs document with far more issues than are found in the typical journal P&L statement. The terms and conditions of the author's contract significantly impact certain elements in the P&L statement.

Table 4.8 is a traditional P&L statement for a new 256-page hardcover black-and-white book with no illustrations, photographs, or statistical tables; it has a realistic print run of 1,000 copies. It could be for a university press or a commercial scholarly publisher.

Table 4.8 SAMPLE PROFIT AND LOSS STATEMENT: SCHOLARLY HB BOOK

Assumptions: 256-page black-and-white book; no photographs, illustrations, or statistical tables

Print run	1,000 copies	
Free copies	100	(author, editor, publishing house)
Gross sales	900 copies	
Copies shipped	771 copies	
Returns	171 copies	(19.00% return rate; industry "average" for scholarly publishers)
Net sales	600 copies	(66.67% sell-through rate of total gross sales)
Never shipped	129 copies	(14.33% of total gross sales)
Suggested retail price	$60.00	("Average" SRP for a humanities book)
Average discount	20%	($48.00 @ net to publisher; "typical" discount rate)
PPB	$4,500.00	($4.50 per unit × 1,000 copies)
Plant	$1,000.00	("Average" for a 256-page book)
Author's advance	$1,000.00	(This is an advance against any future royalty payment earned through the sale of the book)
Royalty rate	10%	(Of net price after 500 copies sold [$4.80 per copy after minimum sales threshold is reached])

Table 4.8 CONTINUED

REVENUES			
1. Total sales	$37,008.00		(771 copies × $48.00 each)
2. Returns	$8,208.00		(171 returned copies × $48.00 each)
3. Net sales	$28,800.00		(#1 − #2 = #3)
Other publishing income	Author's percent		Publisher's percent
Subrights			
Reprints	$0	50% ($0)	50% ($0)
Book club	$0	50% ($0)	50% ($0)
First serial	$0	90% ($0)	70% ($0)
Foreign rights	$0	50% ($0)	50% ($0)
Total	$0	50% ($0)	50% ($0)
COST OF GOODS SOLD (COGS)			
4. PPB	$4,500.00		
5. Plant	$1,000.00		
6. Advance and earned royalty	$1,480.00		($1,000.00 advance; and 10% royalty of net price of $48.00 × 100 sold units; no royalty on the sale of the first 500 sold copies)
7. Royalty write-off	$0.00		(Difference between advance and earned royalty)
8. Total COGS	$6,980.00		(#4 + #5 + #6 + #7 = #8)
9. Initial gross margin	$21,820.00		(#3 − #8 = #9)

Continued

Table 4.8 CONTINUED

10. Other publishing income	$0	(Publishers' share of foreign rights)
11. Initial gross margin	$21,820.00	(#9 + #10 = #11)
12. Inventory write-off	$2,094.00	($6.98 × 300 copies; COGS #8 divided by print run of 1,000 = $6.98; 171 returned copies and 129 never shipped = 300 copies × $6.98)
13. Final gross margin	$19,726.00	(#11 – #12 = #13)
CORPORATE CHARGES		
14. Marketing	$1,000.00	("Average" for a book in the humanities)
15. Overhead 20%	$5,760	("Average" 20% of net sales of $28,800)
16. Net profit	$12,966.00	(#13 – #14 – #15 = #16; 45.02% of net sales)

Source: Author's profit and loss statement with another publisher, not Oxford University Press.

"Gross sales" is generally calculated as 99% of the 1,000 print run; 1% is deducted from the print run as 100 "free copies" allocated for internal use, copies given to the author (generally between 6 and 10 copies), units submitted for book awards, etc. This total can include "dinked" (i.e., damaged) copies, perhaps a torn dust jacket. This total (900 copies) shows what a publisher could sell if all of the books were sold.

"Copies shipped" is the publisher's estimate of the number of units it expects to "sell" (i.e., ship; 771 copies) to various retailers (bookstores, book chains, etc.), distributors, and so forth in what is typically a business-to-business (B-2-B) transaction. Almost every book is "sold" on consignment, which means the publisher has to estimate the number of copies that will be "sold" and returned for a full credit (in this P&L statement 171 copies), assuming the publisher's terms and conditions of sale are followed by the retailer or distributor.

This book had "net sales" of 600 copies, for a 66.67% sell-through rate. Books "never shipped" (i.e., 129 units) are copies that remain in a warehouse and are never shipped to a bookstore or distributor.

This book has an SRP of $60.00, which is a typical SRP for a book in the humanities, perhaps an English literature title analyzing the British Romantic poets (Bryon, Shelley, Keats, Wordsworth, and Coleridge). In the United States, a bookstore can charge whatever it wants for a book—including the SRP, a price higher than the SRP, and a discounted price. Books are almost always sold at a discount to retailers and distributors; the publisher determines the discount rate that is published in a catalog, stated on a website, and so forth. This book has a 20% "discount rate" (which is typical for many scholarly books published by university presses), netting the publisher $48.00 for each unit sold.

"PPB" was $4.50 per copy, for a total of $4,500.00. PPB is based on per unit costs of paper, printing, and binding, which can vary if there is a paper shortage or the book is successful and sells all available copies, triggering a second printing. "Plant" costs include fixed costs to prepare a book for publishing, including (but not limited to) editorial, art, permissions, design, proofs, typesetting, and copyediting. Plant costs are usually one-time expenditures regardless of whether the run is 500 or 9,500.

The author received an "author's advance" of $1,000.00, which is an advance payment against any future royalty earnings. The "royalty rate" was 10% of net publisher revenues (i.e., $4.80 per copy sold) after the publisher sold 500 copies (and returns were factored into the final sale total of 500 units). This provision allowed the publisher to recoup expenses before paying any royalty. Some authors receive a "step royalty," perhaps 5% for the first 500 copies sold, 7% for sales between 501 and 999 units, and 10% for +1,000 copies.

"Gross sales" are actual sales, calculated at 771 copies at $48 per copy, for a total of $37,008. "Returns" were 171 at $48 each for $8,208. Net sales were 600 units (i.e., gross sales of 771 minus returns of 171) for $28,800 (i.e., 600 copies times $48 per copy). There was no additional income from rights or reprints.

An important item is the "cost of goods sold" (COGS). It includes PPB ($4,500.00), plant ($1,000), and the author's "advance" ($1,000) and "earned royalty" ($480). There was no "royalty write-off," which occurs when the author's royalty advance is greater than the royalty earned plus the author's share of reprints, rights, or subrights. The total cost of goods sold was $6,980.00.

The "final gross margin" was $19,726.00 (i.e., gross margin of $21,820.00 minus "inventory write-off" of $2,094.00).

Every publishing operation has "corporate charges," that is, actual expenditures. "Marketing" includes all advertising, promotion, and publicity costs to promote a title. It is generally a specific dollar amount times the number of copies printed, in this case $1,000.00 (i.e., $1.00 for each printed copy). "Generic marketing" is usually non-title-specific promotion costs such as catalogs (which are D-2-C), seasonal ads (which can generate possibly better margins since they bypass retailer discounts), and conference booth displays. "Co-Op" marketing dollars (i.e., co-operative advertising dollars) are funds provided directly to booksellers or internet websites selling books based on their book purchasing patterns. In essence, the more a bookstore or book chain on an internet site purchases books from a publisher, the more the store or chain or website receives toward "co-op" advertising in a store's newspaper ads, catalogs, radio or television ads, displays, point-of-purchase materials, book cover display on website, etc. Very few university presses can afford "co-op" programs.

"Corporate overhead" is the book's share of corporate (sometimes divisional) costs, which generally include corporate (or divisional) expenses for salaries, benefits, supplies, travel, computers, enterprise software, office space, rent, utilities, phone, internet, and so forth. This is an accounting metric to evaluate the total indirect costs to create the book. It can also include freight costs from the printer to the warehouse, and freight expenditures from the warehouse to retailers or distributors. This calculation is often done by a publisher's (or an imprint's) "business manager."

A significant number of titles are released in both printed and e-book versions because of the interest in digital products among academics, researchers, students, and libraries. Table 4.10 is the e-book version of the same hardcover book analyzed in Table 4.9. The basic assumptions for the e-book are very similar to the hardcover title. It will be a 256-page black-and-white e-book, again with no photographs, illustrations, or statistical tables. The book will also have an SRP of $60.00 and sell 600 copies (the same as the printed book), and it will be sold directly by the publisher on its website (a D-2-C option), which can generate higher margins than the printed book.

Total "net sales" revenue topped $60,000.00 for the e-books (versus $36,000.00 for the printed book). There was no "return," so gross and net sales tallies were the same. "Plant" was again $1,000.00 since these operations are necessary for the e-book. There was no "PPB." The "advance" remained at $1,000.00, but the royalty rate was 10% of $60.00 (generating $600.00 versus $480.00 for the printed version) for all copies sold in excess of the 500-unit level. There was no "royalty write-off." And "total COGS" reached $2,600.00 (versus $6,980.00 for the printed book).

The "initial gross margin" was $33,400; there was no "other publishing income" or "inventory write-off"; and the "final gross margin" was also $33,400.00.

Table 4.9 SAMPLE PROFIT AND LOSS STATEMENT: SCHOLARLY E-BOOK VERSION OF BOOK LISTED IN TABLE 4.9

Assumptions for the e-book: 256-page black-and-white e-book; no photographs, illustrations, or statistical tables. Sold directly by the publisher on the publisher's website at the SRP of $60.00. Author received $1,000.00 advance against royalty and a 10% royalty rate after 500 copies were sold.

REVENUES		
1. Gross sales	$36,000.00	(600 copies × $60)
2. Returns	$0	
3. Net sales	$36,000.00	(#1 – #2 = #3)
COST OF GOODS SOLD (COGS)		
4. Plant	$1,000.00	(Same as the printed book)
5. PPB	$0	(No PPB for the digital book)
6. Advance and royalty	$1,600.00	($1,000.00 advance and 10% of SRP after 500 copies sold; 100 units @ $6.00 = $600)
7. Royalty write-off	$0	
8. Total COGS	$2,600	(#4 + #5 + #6 + #7 = #8)
9. Initial gross margin	$33,400.00	(#3 – #8 = #9)

Table 4.9 CONTINUED

10. Other publishing income	$0	(No other income)
11. Final gross margin	$33,400.00	(#9 – #10 = #11)
12. Inventory write-off	$0	
13. Final gross return	$33,400.00	(#11 – #12 = #13)
CORPORATE CHARGES		
14. Marketing	$1,000.00	(Various costs for catalogs, trade shows, etc.)
15. Overhead 30%*	$10,800.00	(30% of net sales)
16. Net profit	$21,600.00	(#13 – #14 – #15 = #16; 60.00% of net sales)

*Overhead assumes additional costs to the publisher for swipe fees and web server expenses.

Marketing stayed at $1,000.00. However, "corporate overhead" was 30% ($10,800.00) versus 20% ($5,760.00) for the printed book because of additional costs associated with web server expenses and "swipe fees" (i.e., the transaction fee the publisher pays to the credit card company when the sale is made).

The e-book posted a net profit of $21,600.00 (versus $12,966.00 for the printed book), generating a 60% margin (it was 45.02% for the printed title). This means that the author ended up with $2,600.00 for the e-book and only $1,480 for the printed version ($1,120 more). The publisher recorded a net profit or "surplus" for the e-book of an additional $8,634.00, which indicates clearly why many scholarly book publishers emphasize (or should emphasize) digital versions.

NOTES

1. Ian Gadd, *The History of Oxford University Press*, vol. 1, *Beginnings to 1780* (Oxford: Oxford University Press, 2014); Simon Eliot, *The History of Oxford University Press*, vol. 2, *1780 to 1896* (Oxford: Oxford University Press, 2014); W. Roger Louis, *The History of Oxford University Press*, vol. 3, *1896 to 1970* (Oxford: Oxford University Press, 2014); Keith Robbins, *The History of Oxford University Press*, vol. 4, *1970–2004* (Oxford: Oxford University Press, 2017); Angus Phillips and Michael Bhaskar, eds., *The Oxford Handbook of Publishing* (Oxford: Oxford University Press 2019), 1–10. David McKitterick, *A History of Cambridge University Press*, vol. 1, *Printing and the Book Trade in Cambridge, 1534–1698* (Cambridge: Cambridge University Press, 1992); David McKitterick, *A History of Cambridge University Press*, vol. 2, *Scholarship and Commerce, 1698–1872* (Cambridge: Cambridge University Press, 1998); David McKitterick, *A History of Cambridge University Press*, vol. 3, *New Worlds for Learning, 1873–1972* (Cambridge: Cambridge University Press, 2004). The debate over which one of these presses was the first scholarly book publisher has been the subject of great debate between those who insist that the first press was started at Oxford by Caxton in 1478 and those who maintain that the legal creation of the first university press was at Cambridge when it received the "letters patent" from King Henry VIII in 1534 and the university published its first book in 1584. Cambridge also holds the "letters patent" as the Monarch's printer. In any case, Oxford and Cambridge are superior scholarly book publishers.
2. Cecile M. Jagodzinski, "The University Press in North America: A Brief History," *Journal of Scholarly Publishing* 40, 1 (October 2008): 1. Also see Sue Ann Gardner, "Scholarly Publishing in the U.S., Then and Now: A Brief History and Implications for the Future," http://digitalcommons.unl.edu/library_talks/81. Sandy Thatcher, "A Brief History of Scholarly Publishing," http://pu65.org/album/50th%20Reunion%20Essays/thatcher.pdf; Sebastien Liarte, "Academic Publishing: Past and Future," www.doi.org/10.3917/mana.16500739.
3. Association of University Presses (AUP), http://www.aupresses.org/about-aaup/about-university-pterddrd/history-of-university-presses. The Association of American University Presses (AAUP) was established in 1937; in December 2017, it changed its name to AUP.

4. Association of University Presses (AUP), http://www.aupresses.org/about-aaup/about-university-pterddrd/history-of-university-presses.
5. Jagodzinski, "The University Press in North America: A Brief History," 4.
6. Joseph S. Meisel,. "American University Presses, 1929–1979: Adaptation and Evolution," *Book History* 13 (2010): 122–127.
7. Donald P. Bean, *American Scholarly Publishing* (Chicago: mimeograph manuscript, 1929).
8. August Fruge, *A Skeptic Among Scholars: August Fruge on University Publishing* (Berkeley, Los Angeles, and London: University of California Press, 1993), 35. Also see Marsh Jeanneret, *God and Mammon: Universities as Publishers* (Urbana and Chicago: University of Illinois Press, 1989), 25–29. Also see Alison Mudditt, "The Past, Present, and Future of American University Presses: A View From the Left Coast," https://onlinelibrary.wiley.com/doi/full/10.1002/leap.1047; Richard Abel, "The National Enquiry Into Scholarly Communication—Twenty Years After," *Publishing Research Quarterly* 15, 1 (Spring 1999): 3–19; Robert B. Townsend, "History and the Future of Scholarly Publishing," https://www.historians.org/publications-and-dictories/perspectives-on-history/october-2003/history-and-the-future-of-scholarly-publishing.
9. John Tebbel, *Between Covers: The Rise and Transformation of American Book Publishing* (New York: Oxford University Press, 1987), 333.
10. Ibid., 334.
11. Bennett Cerf, *At Random: The Reminiscences of Bennett Cerf* (New York: Random House, 2012), 99–122. Also see Bettye H. Pruitt, *The Making of Harcourt General: A History of Growth Through Diversification, 1922–1992* (Boston: Harvard Business School Press, 1994), xi, 220–222, 225.
12. Tebbel, *Between Covers: The Rise and Transformation of American Book Publishing*, 334.
13. Ibid. Also see John Tebbel, *A History of Book Publishing in the United States*, vol. 3 (New York: R. R. Bowker, 1978), 597–598.
14. Association of University Presses (AUP), http://www.aupresses.org/about-aaup/history.
15. Michael E. Porter, *Competitive Strategy: Techniques for Analyzing Industries and Competitors* (New York: Free Press, 1998), 47–75. Also see Michael E. Porter, "What Is Strategy?," *Harvard Business Review* 74, 6 (November–December 1996): 61–78. Analyses of consolidation in the commercial sector include J. Kendrick Noble, "Mergers and Acquisitions of Professional and Scholarly Publishers: A Contrarian View," *Book Research Quarterly* 5, 3 (September 1989): 45–50; Kathleen Robertson, "Mergers, Acquisitions, and Access: STM Publishing Today," *Library and Information Services in Astronomy* 4 (July 2–5, 2002): 95–102; Aileen Fyfe, Kelly Coate, Stephen Curry, Stuart Lawson, Noah Moxham, and

Camilla Mork Rostvik, "Untangling Academic Publishing: A History of the Relationship Between Commercial Interests, Academic Prestige, and the Circulation of Research," http://eprints.rclis.org/31498; Raf Guns, "Concentration of Academic Book Publishers," https://openaccess.leidenuniv.nl/bitstream/handle/1887/65268/STI2018_paper_95.pdf?sequence=1; Elin B. Christianson, "Mergers in the Publishing Industry, 1958–1970," *Journal of Library History* 7, 1 (January 1972): 5–32; John Sutherland, "Publishing History: A Hole at the Centre of Literary Sociology," *Critical Inquiry* 14, 3 (Spring 1988): 574–589.

16. Elaine Maisner, "Getting Published by a University Press," https://www.historians.org/publications-and-diretories/perspectives=on-the-history/may-2002/getting-published=by-a-university-press. Also see Margaret Stieg Dalton, "The Publishing Experiences of Historians," *Journal of Scholarly Publishing* 39, (April 2008): 197–240; Paul Parsons, *Getting Published: The Acquisition Process at University Presses* (Knoxville: University of Tennessee Press, 1989), 7–16; Lewis A. Coser, Charles Kadushin, and Walter W. Powell, *Books: The Culture and Commerce of Publishing* (New York: Basic Books, 1982), 97–147; Jacques Barzun, *On Writing, Editing, and Publishing: Essays, Explicative, and Hortatory* (Chicago: University of Chicago Press, 1980), 103–114; Richard E. Abel and Lyman W. Newlin, eds., *Scholarly Publishing: Books, Journals, Publishers, and Libraries in the Twentieth Century* (New York: John Wiley & Sons, 2002), 29–46; Robin P. Peek and Gregory B. Newby, eds., *Scholarly Publishing: The Electronic Frontier* (Cambridge, MA: MIT Press 1996), 3–16; Robin Derricourt, *An Author's Guide to Scholarly Publishing* (Princeton, NJ: Princeton University Press, 1996), 41–62.
17. To gauge and understand the diverse channels of distribution, the author conducted a series of interviews with representatives in the university press, commercial scholarly publishing sector, and trade book industry.
18. Katherine Daniel, Joseph Esposito, and Roger C, Schonfeld, "Library Acquisition Patterns," https://sr.ithaka.org/wp-content/uploads/2019/01/SR-Report-2018-Library-Acquisition-Patterns-01292019.pdf.
19. Ibid., 22.
20. Ibid., 20.
21. Ibid., 20. Also see Kate Dohl, Babak Hamidzadeh, and Ben Wallberg, "Doing More. With More: Academic Libraries, Digital Services, and Revenue Generation," https://sr.ithaka.org/wp-content/uploads/2019/01/SR-Issue-Brief-doing-more=with-nore-01242019.pdf; Publishers Communication Group, "Library Budget Predictions for 2017," http://www.pcgplus.com/wp-content/uploads/2017/05/Library-Budget-Predictions-for-2017-public.pdf; Constance Malpas, "Cloud-Sourcing

Research Collections: Managing Print in the Mass-Digitized Library Environment," http://www.oclc.org/research/publications/library/2011/2011-01.pdf; Dawn Hall, *Shared Collections: Collaborative Stewardship* (Chicago: American Library Association, 2016), 77–90.

22. Association of Departments of English, "A Changing Major: The Report of the 2016–17 ADE Ad Hoc Committee on the English Major," https://www.ade.mla.org/Resources/Reports-and-Other-Resources/A-Changing-Major-The-Report-of-the-2016-17-ADE-Ad-Hoc-Committee-on-the-English-Major. The report stated that there was a "precipitous decline in undergraduate English majors across North America that began around 2009."
23. Lewis G. Liu, Harold Gee, and Charles Terng, "Exploring the Determinants of Scholarly Book Prices in the Fields of Science, Technology, and Medicine," *Library Trends* 67, 2 (Fall 2018): 255–285. Also see Ryan L. Phillips, "Book Citations in Ph.D. Science Dissertations: An Examination of Commercial Book Publishers' Influence," *Library Trends* 67, 2 (Fall 2018): 286–302; Joel Waldfogel and Imke Reimers, "Storming the Gatekeepers: Digital Disintermediation in the Market for Books," *Information Economics and Policy* 31 (2015): 47–58; Alexander Serenko, Nick Bontis, and Madora Moshonsky, "Books as a Knowledge Translation Mechanism: Citation Analysis and Author Survey," *Journal of Knowledge Management* 16, 3 (2012): 495–511; K. Nageswara Rao, Manorama Tripathi, and Sunil Kumar, "Cost of Print and Digital Books: A Comparative Study," *Journal of Academic Librarianship* 42, 4 (2016): 445–452; Tina P. Franks and Daniel S. Dotson, "Book Publishers Cited in Science Dissertations: Are Commercial Publishers Worth the Hype?," *Science & Technology Libraries* 36, 1 (2017): 63–76.
24. Joyce Kachergis, *One Book/Five Ways: The Publishing Procedures of Five University Presses* (Chicago: University of Chicago Press, 1994), vii. The data in this book was from the 1977 presentation.
25. Ibid. Information about the following university presses: Chicago, pp. 40–41, 44; MIT, 109–112; North Carolina, 162–166; Texas, 226–229; and Toronto, 272–275.
26. Nancy Maron, Kimberly Schmelzinger Christine Mulhern, and Daniel Rossman, "The Costs of Publishing Monographs: Toward a Transparent Methodology," *Journal of Electronic Publishing* 19, 1 (Summer 2016): 28, http://quod.lib.umich.edu/jep/333645100019.103?view=text;rgn=main.
27. University of Chicago, ed., *The Chicago Manual of Style*, 17th ed. (Chicago and London: University of Chicago Press, 2017), 59–77.
28. United States Copyright Office, "Circulars," https://www.copyright.gov/circs. This website lists 35 circulars on "The Foundations of Copyright" as

well as 12 documents related to "Performing Arts Works," 9 on "Literary Works," and 5 on "Licensing." Also see *The Chicago Manual of Style*, Chapter 4, on "Rights, Permissions, and Copyright Administration," 171–219.

29. CIROBE, http://www.CIROBE.com.
30. American Arbitration Association, https://www.adr.org: "The American Arbitration Association (AAA) handles the out-of-court resolution of a dispute between parties to a contract, decided by an impartial third party (the arbitrator)—is faster and more cost effective than litigation. AAA cases are often settled prior to the arbitrator's decision—and nearly half of those cases incur no arbitrator compensation."

[5]

THE CHANGING WORLD OF SCHOLARLY BOOKS

The Impact of Technology, Money Flows, Open Access, and Libraries as Publishers

INTRODUCTION: IMPACT OF CHANGES IN TECHNOLOGIES ON SCHOLARLY BOOKS

Digital scholarly book technologies, especially print-on-demand (POD), directly impacted authors, readers, libraries, and publishers. It was possible to significantly reduce traditional lithographic (often called litho, offset, or photo-offset) print runs and rely on small runs, which were more likely to be sold, and then utilize POD for additional sales.[1]

In addition, it was now possible for authors to undertake research utilizing remote access to digital library journal and book holdings (as well as working with colleagues in different parts of the world). This was essentially an efficient way to undertake some, but clearly not all, basic research activities. However, the availability of digital databases placed a strain, both physically and financially, on libraries as they attempted to keep up to date with the availability of data aggregators (e.g., Project Muse, Elsevier, Oxford University Press, etc.).[2]

Some industry technology experts predicted the death of the printed book, or printed journal, stressing the "inevitable" transformation of scholarly communications away from a costly print-oriented format to a less expensive digital "e-book" or "e-journal" format. Marilyn Deegan wrote that "the future of the academic book is at a crossroads. . . . Researchers on the 'Academic Book of the Future' project are recommending that academics and publishers work together to develop a new vision that embraces technology and focuses on enhancing the reader experience."[3] While digital scholarly formats grew in importance in the journal sector, books remained, for the most part, a printed product; the outlook for the foreseeable future seems to indicate that printed books will continue to be the primary format.

Now academics, researchers, or students with a laptop, tablet, or smartphone can read through decades' worth of scholarly materials without visiting a library. There were stumbling blocks, however. Most journals were locked behind paywalls, and a few (e.g., *Harvard Business Review*) were read-only serials. And some publishers restricted usage access for certain books to one individual at a time. Nonetheless, sharp declines in prices for digital devices with more memory and rather quick access to the internet helped transform the scholarly publishing industry.[4]

Academic libraries (and in fact all libraries) pay a great deal of attention to collection development, which is an important and costly endeavor based on the "just-in-case" strategy; in essence, this is a dual-sided uncertainty situation. The library is not sure if a specific title will be needed by faculty members or students, and vice versa. For example, the Cornell University Library (CUL) reported that "approximately 45% of print monographs in the CUL collection published since 1990 have circulated at least once to date; approximately 55% of these [print monographs] have never circulated."[5]

Cornell's experience of titles that never circulate over long periods of time has been, unfortunately, a problem that has plagued most academic libraries. This situation sparked the development of a change in the circulation management strategy at many academic libraries, the adoption of the patron-driven acquisition (PDA) model (sometimes called a demand driven process [DDA]). Now a library can list a title in its digital or print catalog but not necessarily purchase the title. If a faculty member of a student requests the book, the library can either buy the book or determine if it can utilize interlibrary to get access, for a short period of time, for the reader. A by-product of this shift in strategy triggered decreases in library purchases of printed books, which was the goal of PDA.

Rebecca Schroeder, Tom Wright, and Robert Murdoch viewed PDA positively, as did many librarians:

> Patron driven acquisitions is a collection development tool that shifts a library's purchasing decision from a librarian "just-in-case" decision to a patron "just-in time" decision. It is a way for students, faculty, and staff to decide what the library buys. It is a plan where bibliographic records are added to the library's catalog and made available to patrons. As patrons discover and access them, a purchase is triggered. . . . Purchasing on demand shifts library funds from speculative buying to buying what is wanted and with e-books there is immediate access for the patron.[6]

Edward A. Goedeken and Karen G. Lawson also supported the efficiency of PDA:

> The challenge of creating an effective and appropriate library collection has been further tested by the recent advent of what Clayton Christensen has termed "disruptive technology." . . . For Christensen, technology can either be sustaining or disruptive. Sustaining technologies improve the performance of products and continue to make them valuable to the consumer. Disruptive technologies, on the other hand, initially underperform in the marketplace, but have a tendency to improve their quality at a rapid rate and eventually replace the established

> technology. . . . For libraries, the availability of electronic books (e-books) that can be accessed outside of the traditional catalog via a patron-driven or demand-driven process (DDA) is indeed disruptive to the entire fabric of established collection development procedures.[7]

David C. Tyler, Christina D. Falci, Joyce C. Melvin, and Anita M. Kreps analyzed PDA, and they came to the conclusion that "numerous publications on patron-driven acquisition (PDA) for print books and similar materials have reported that patron requested materials circulate more."[8]

The increased availability of digital e-book bundles, from various aggregators, was a significant opportunity for these libraries to reduce printed book expenditures (and shelving time and shelf space) and has, in certain instances, enabled multiple simultaneous users of a specific title. However, some aggregators offered costly bundles, sometimes filled with titles of little interest (sometimes called "chunking") for some librarians because their university did not offer academic degree programs in certain areas (e.g., nursing, pharmacy, medicine); others stipulated that only one individual at a time could access certain titles, which was not well received by some librarians and their faculty members; and some faculty members and students just preferred printed books.[9]

Another substantive trend that negatively impacted library book purchases was the emphasis of placing book chapters (or in some instances entire books) on electronic library reserves (called "e-reserves"). This practice, designed to make more scholarly content available for free to students, has significantly eroded the market for individual scholarly book purchases.[10]

Anne E. Bromley wrote about a related example involving the University of Virginia Library and the University of Virginia Press. They announced in 2019 that they created "Aperio," their new digital publishing partnership that "employs the latest technology to produce what's called 'open access' to research scholarship and other educational materials—eventually including textbooks."[11]

A number of scholarly book publishers, both university presses and commercial publishers, are active in the higher education textbook sector, because the margins are very attractive; however, this book category faces severe market pressures. According to the National Association of College Stores (NACS), about 25% of all higher education textbook sales go to the used book business.[12] Other major concerns about this market segment center on two substantive issues. The first one is the importation of textbooks printed and published legally in foreign nations, which was deemed to be allowed because of the US Supreme Court's majority opinion by Justice Breyer in the 2013 Kirtsaeng decision.[13] The second one deals with pirated e-textbook downloads.

THE "DARK" SIDE OF TECHNOLOGY: BOOK PIRACY

Matthew Jones wrote that "e-book piracy is on the rise across the board, in 2018 +800 million e-book downloads were recorded, but academic publishers are particularly vulnerable. Piracy is estimated to cost academic publishers around 28% of potential sales. The high prices of academic books tend to incentivize piracy by students, and DRM technology is difficult to enforce."[14] Judith Rosen wrote in *Publishers Weekly* on February 18, 2019, that "free materials—borrowed, shared, or downloaded—are also eating into textbook sales. According to the NACS Student Watch biannual survey of the 2017–2018 academic year, the share of students using free materials went from 19% in spring 2016 to 32% in spring 2018."[15]

Scholarly books are expensive. So, some academics and students look to buy a less expensive version of a title. For example, Harvard University Press published *A Democracy at War: America's Homefront at Home and Abroad in World War II* by William O'Neill. The suggested retail price (SRP) for the hardcover was listed (in February 2019) at $44.75, the paperback version was $30.43, and the used copy of the hardcover was $8.17. These new and used options are rather typical since the online used book market is rather efficient, often using "dynamic prices" (i.e., the online price is dynamic—it can change within seconds based on supply and demand). Pricing concerns prompted many individuals to consider other options, some of which are patently not legal.

While better known as the largest piracy website for pirated academic journals, Sci-Hub's piracy of 1 million-plus books triggered intense discussions among book publishing companies and trade associations about trying to combat this unbelievable loss of sales revenue. Access to Sci-Hub, or some of the other pirated book sites, enables an individual to find and download illegally in less than 10 seconds, depending on the individual's access to the internet, a complete scholarly book. The Association of American Publishers (AAP), along with other publisher associations, has worked with the International Intellectual Property Alliance (IIPA) to inform citizens, and various governmental department and offices, about the pernicious impact of piracy on the livelihoods of authors and individuals working in book publishing firms. The AAP's statements on piracy have been presented to the US Congress, especially congressional committees that address changes to the US copyright law, regarding the fact that the

> health and competitiveness of the U.S. economy depends on a thriving copyright sector that creates revenue, jobs and exports. However, many AAP member-publishers who sell to global markets face inadequate or limited copyright protections abroad, as well as persistent online and hard goods copyright infringement (aka "piracy"). The lack of adequate copyright protection and enforcement make it difficult to deter infringement and hamper a publisher's ability to compete on equal footing in these markets.[16]

Digimarc and Nielsen estimated that book piracy costs US publishers about $315 million annually in lost revenues.[17] In a related study, “Inside the Mind of a Book Pirate,” Nielsen and Digimarc undertook a sample of 595 individuals who had pirated books. The findings are revealing and indicate the basic problems in confronting book piracy: “The majority of illegal [book] downloaders are 18 to 34 years old, educated, and wealthy. . . . Roughly 30% of illegal downloaders either obtain their content from friends, via email, or flash drive, or from downloading from public/open torrent sites.”[18]

Drilling down into the datasets, Nielsen and Digimarc discovered that 40% of illegal downloaders graduated from college, with 32% having a graduate degree; 36% had an annual income between $50,000 and $99,000; and 29% earned more than $100,000. As for motivation, 58% indicated that illegal downloads were convenient or easy.[19] So, these individuals were well educated and were not poor students in developing nations who needed access to intellectual content to complete an education. The demographic characteristics seemed to undermine a few open access (OA) arguments and certain support for the need for a Sci-Hub website to help make content more readily available for individuals who cannot afford pricy books.

This is why it is remarkably difficult to combat piracy, since digital books are so easy to find, replicate, or post on an online “dark web” website, a key issue addressed by Imke Reimers. “Efforts to prevent such piracy have mostly been public in nature, with mixed results. . . . [Book] publishing houses have increasingly hired private firms in an attempt to limit the amount of online book piracy.”[20]

A well-publicized and rather successful event, sponsored by the Association of College and Research Libraries (ACRL) is the “Fair Use/Fair Dealing Week,” which seeks to generate awareness of the “fair use” clause of the US copyright law (§107) at US colleges. Fair Use/Fair Dealing Week is “an annual celebration of fair use and fair dealing. It is designed to highlight and promote the opportunities presented by fair use and fair dealing, celebrate successful stories, and explain these doctrines.”[21]

However, in spite of rigorous copyright laws in the United States (and elsewhere), printed book piracy has been a tremendous problem for several centuries, negatively impacting both US authors and leading European writers.[22] In essence, book pirates are like roaches: get rid of one, and 10 more appear. However, this is a battle that must be fought, or the number of pirated books could start to mount up in an industry that can ill afford massive annual financial losses.

CHANGES IN MONEY FLOWS

The vast majority of university presses, unlike the commercial ones, have relatively small book revenue streams, about $300 million in the United States (if you exclude the revenues of Oxford and Cambridge). However, a relatively small cluster of university presses have journal revenues (e.g., Toronto, Johns Hopkins), and an even smaller number handle book warehousing and distribution services for smaller presses (e.g., Chicago and Oxford). Hopkins also houses Project Muse, which generates a positive cash flow for Hopkins.

The research of Nancy Maron, Kimberly Schmelzinger, Christine Mulhern, and Daniel Rossman addressed a number of important issues, including university press revenues.[23] Members of the Association of University Presses (AUP), with the exception of Oxford and Cambridge, are placed into four revenue categories; the number of presses in any group can change annually, and all percentages were rounded off and may not always equal 100%: Group 1, revenues up to $1.5 million—generally about 42% of the presses are in this group; Group 2, $1.5 million to $3 million—about 22%; Group 3, $3 million to $6 million—about 24%; and Group 4, over $5 million—about 13%. This categorization enables AUP to generate a series of important financial documents for their members; Oxford and Cambridge are excluded because of their size, and their tallies would skew averages within Group 4 (and total annual revenues for all four groups).

Chapter 4 had details regarding the various channels of distribution for university press books. While there has been a shift, and a dramatic shift, in certain sales in the channels, the most intriguing ones involved academic libraries and the exportation of scholarly books. Table 5.1 has sales data from academic libraries (which are more important than public library purchases of academic books). Between 2001 and 2017, total expenditures of academic libraries decreased about 30.62%. While this statistic is at best unsettling since academics and students rely on college and university libraries, the statistic for the purchase of books was frightful, declining 74.81%. This means that the percentage of books purchased in 2001 was 20.94% but only 7.6% in 2017.

All of the large commercial scholarly book publishers, and a small but significant cluster of university presses (e.g., Yale, Princeton, Oxford), are involved directly in printed book exports and imports. The best source of highly reliable data on exports and imports is the US Department of Commerce and International Trade Administration (ITA). Based on numerous and detailed conversations (between 1998 and 2019) with representatives at the ITA, university press directors and business managers, and experts in the surety bond business[24] (which works closely with the US Department of Homeland Security), it is clear that the ITA datasets pose a slight methodological problem. First, because of the "Harmonized Tariff System" (HTS),[25] the ITA comingles technical, scientific, and professional books into one category. It is highly likely that this category includes most if not all university press books since this book category is not listed in the HTS documents. Second, because of US tariff regulations, imports are rather carefully monitored by the ITA, and the surety bond underwriters, probably capturing +95% of imports (based on discussions with surety bond executives since 2008). Third, book exports are not regulated by well-established tariff laws and rules, and, traditionally, the ITA closely monitored exports beyond a certain minimum dollar threshold (which is approximately $2,500, although it can change this amount). This means that the ITA estimates, using various statistical sampling techniques, shipments with a dollar value below the minimum threshold. The concept of "monitoring exports closely" is intriguing since discussions with the

Table 5.1 ACADEMIC LIBRARY ACQUISITIONS EXPENDITURES, 2001–2017: BOOKS

Year	*Total Expenditures*	*Book Expenditures*	*Book Percent of Total Expenditures*
2001	$1,358,969,601	$284,635,850	20.94%
2002	$1,443,102,475	$292,189,789	20.25%
2003	$1,352,674,991	$267,260,940	19.76%
2004	$1,429,793,005	$261,373,022	18.28%
2005	$1,363,013,834	$237,871,915	17.45%
2006	$739,643,639	$112,374,681	15.19%
2007	$960,876,102	$145,018,384	15.09%
2008	$1,163,695,836	$137,645,878	11.83%
2009	$870,146,267	$101,903,189	11.71%
2010	$1,075,146,358	$130,299,026	12.12%
2011	$1,074,282,010	$128,147,757	11.93%
2012	$1,088,781,751	$124,217,024	11.41%
2013	$1,159,993,119	$115,938,131	9.99%
2014	$1,165,136,885	$101,706,308	8.73%
2015	$1,139,269,827	$88,019,968	7.73%
2016	$1,052,205,647	$80,598,953	7.66%
2017	$942,878,213	$71,687,817	7.60%

N.B. Based on statistical data from various sources; the datasets are for an academic year; so, for example, 2002 represents expenditures for the 2001–2002 academic year.

Source: *The Bowker Annual; The Library and Book Trade Almanac*, various years.

ITA failed to ascertain with any precision how "closely" small export book shipments were "monitored."[26]

Between 2001 and 2017, printed book exports in this HTS system declined 41.41%. This total does not include the sale of rights or e-books. In the years after 1998, unsuccessful attempts were undertaken by various US book trade associations (e.g., the Book Industry Study Group) to obtain some data on the total value of rights. So, it is likely that the export totals are too low because of ITA estimates of book exports as well as the growth in the rights business in New York City (Book Export and the Rights Fair), London, Frankfurt, etc. Book imports also posted declines between 2001 and 2017 (−17.15%), impacted by a number of economic factors including the recession of 2007, currency conversion issues, etc. Table 5.2 has the details.

All scholarly publishers have to work within defined budgets. While commercial publishers are expected to turn a profit at the end of either a calendar or a fiscal year, university presses, for the most part, cannot generate a "profit" because they are, at least in the United States, deemed to be "nonprofit" entities by the US Internal Revenue Service (IRS) under section 501(c)(3) of the tax code.[27] They can have a "surplus" at the end of a year, and these funds have to be used to support the chartable nonprofit activities of the university press.

So, an important revenue stream for university presses, aside from the ones listed in the sample profit and statements in Chapter 4, also includes what is called "parent institution support." The level of this financial support varies significantly, but "typical averages" in 2019 ranged between about $500,000 and about $750,000. Unfortunately, some universities after the recession of 2007–2009[28] sustained financial losses in endowments, tuition income, and/or gifts from friends and alumni.[29] Concerns about revenue streams prompted several universities (e.g., Duquesne University) and a cluster of universities (part of the University Press of New England) to close down their university presses.[30] There was another ripple effect because of the impact of the recent recession. Many university

Table 5.2 US EXPORTS AND IMPORTS OF TECHNICAL, SCIENTIFIC, AND PROFESSIONAL BOOKS (THOUSANDS OF US DOLLARS)

Year	*Export Revenues*	*Import Revenues*
2001	$411,974	$158,486
2002	$376,576	$189,124
2003	$371,129	$225,889
2004	$391,532	$265,561
2005	$475,407	$291,244
2006	$478,336	$249,248
2007	$560,938	$275,844
2009	$434,888	$177,169
2010	$454,001	$198,021
2011	$339,506	$185,265
2012	$311,183	$175,121
2013	$275,743	$162,378
2014	$266,643	$153,236
2015	$258,683	$145,247
2016	$249,546	$138,519
2017	$241,395	$131,302

N.B. The International Trade Administration rounded off all totals, and totals may not always equal 100%.

Source: US Department of Commerce, International Trade Administration, https://www.trade.gov.

presses eschewed attending the big, and expensive, Book Expo event held annually (and usually) in New York City at the Javits Center. Some small presses had to cancel attendance (and fees) for some of the major academic conferences (e.g., the American Economic Association).

THE MOVEMENT FOR GOLD OPEN ACCESS SCHOLARLY BOOKS

Economic concerns, as well as changing interest of journal readers regarding gold OA, prompted many presses to consider offering a "hybrid" book publishing strategy, that is, publishing a book in both print (hardcover and paperback) and digital e-book formats. As with the gold OA scholarly journal movement, European researchers and policymakers took the lead in generating interest in gold OA scholarly books.

Antonia C. Schrader, Alexander Grossman, and Michael Reiche, from Leipzig University of Applied Sciences, wrote that "only certain researchers can actually publish because of high Book Processing Charges (BPCs). . . . For these reasons, our research project aims to develop an ideal and transferable publishing workflow for OA books that is both cost effective and personnel-efficient as well as media-neutral to enable universities to publish their publications as OA."[31] Ellen Collins and Caren Milloy, in "OAPEN-UK Final Report: A Five-Year Study Into Open Access Monograph Publishing in the Humanities and Social Sciences," remarked:

> Our research suggests that, if we want to move towards open access for monographs, change will need to happen in three important areas: attitudes and perceptions; systems, policies and processes; and business models. . . . In line with the objectives and ethos of OAPEN-UK, the recommendations fall into three categories: 1. Supporting informed

> decision-making—by all stakeholders in the scholarly communications process, but especially by researchers who may consider publishing an open access monograph[.] 2. Taking collaborative action—multiple stakeholders working together to overcome challenges or develop new standards[.] 3. Enabling projects, research and experimentation—initiatives to support innovation or deepen understanding . . . [and] [r]eframe the discussions around open access for scholarly monographs by acknowledging that monographs are different from journals. The issues, concerns and opportunities are not necessarily the same as in the journals market and are sometimes more complex or compounded by issues in the wider e-book environment.[32]

Lindsay McKenzie wrote that "last week University College, London Press, Britain's first fully-open-access university press, celebrated a milestone—one million downloads of its free academic books. . . . The popularity of the OA titles is proof that open access is the most effective way to reach a wider, more diverse and global audience."[33] Martin Paul Eve in *Open Access in the Humanities: Contexts, Controversies, and the Future* addressed the importance of economic models for OA books. "Despite the emergence of the BPC as the model of choice for many publishers, several other economic models are appearing (some of which are experimental), including print subsidy, freemium, and consortia."[34]

In the United States, the movement toward OA e-books has been slower than in Europe. However, one of the leaders in the gold OA scholarly monograph movement has been the University of California Press with its Luminos Open Access imprint. As with gold OA journals, California charges a BPC.

> The author will be asked to secure $7,500.00 either from their home institution and/or another independent funding source. . . . This subsidy requirement is for titles of no more than 90,000 words and 25 images. . . . Authors or institutions who don't have

> sufficient funds available to them may be eligible for our Author Waiver Fund.[35]

The American Council of Learned Societies (ACLS), the Andrew W. Mellon Foundation, and the National Endowment for the Humanities (NEH) joined forces to encourage OA e-books. Mellon and NEH "announced seven [OA] grants, totaling more than $1 million, to convert important out-of-print humanities texts into freely available e-books."[36]

In 2017, the Association of American Universities (AAU), the Association of Research Libraries (ARL), and the AUP announced the creation of an open access monograph publishing initiative:

> This new initiative is intended to advance the dissemination of scholarship by humanities and humanistic social sciences faculty members by publishing open-access digital editions of peer-reviewed and professionally edited monographs. Participating universities and colleges have committed to three components: a baseline university publishing grant of $15,000.00 to support the publication of an open-access, digital monograph of 90,000 or less (with additional funding for works of greater length or completely to be negotiated by the author, institution, and publisher); set a target of awarding three publishing grants per year; and participate in this initiative for five years.[37]

Sixty-two presses agreed to participate in this initiative, including Chicago, Georgia, North Texas, Southern Illinois, and Wayne State.

This initiative prompted the AAU, ARL, and AUP to undertake a series of planning sessions, and, because of these discussions, the name of this initiative became "Toward an Open Monograph Ecosystem," or TOME.[38] Peter Berkery, executive director of the AUP, at the July 31, 2018, meeting of TOME provided an update of TOME's activities. Berkery announced that, while TOME is optional, it had received 47 grant applications, 24 grants were awarded, and 28 contract agreements had been signed to publish monographs under the

TOME initiative. Berkery maintained that "authors enjoy benefits of digitized increased discoverability; [this was] a step toward innovation in humanities scholarship . . . [and this initiative had] long-term potential to transform HSS scholarship."[39]

Concerns remain about the progress of OA e-books in the United States, including the dark cloud of piracy, global online sites selling used scholarly books, and the almost inevitable emergence of predatory e-book publishing firms. Yet some of the early studies indicate that OA could address the basic financial issues that plague scholarly publishing firms, specifically discoverability. Springer Nature released a white paper "The OA Effect: How Does Open Access Affect the Usage of Scholarly Books?" This report presented the following conclusions, based on a large research study:

> It is frequently claimed that open access (OA) has the potential to increase usage and citations. This report substantiates such claims for books in particular, through benchmarking the performance of Springer Nature books made OA through the immediate (gold) route against that of equivalent non-OA books. . . . The average performance of OA books, as measured by usage, citations and online mentions for the first four years of each book's life, was compared with the average performance of non-OA titles. We found that Springer Nature OA books perform better than non-OA books published by Springer Nature in all three categories that we assessed: on average, there are just under 30,000 chapter downloads per OA book within the first year of publication, which is 7 times more than for the average non-OA book; citations are on average 50% higher for OA books than for non-OA books, over a four-year period; OA books receive an average of 10 times more online mentions than non-OA books, over a three-year period. . . . Those we spoke with argued that OA is not just a publishing model, but also a means of addressing the issue of equal access to knowledge and ensuring that publicly-funded research is available to all.[40]

ACADEMIC LIBRARIES AS SCHOLARLY BOOK PUBLISHERS AND ADMINISTRATORS OF UNIVERSITY PRESSES

In recent years, there have been two major developments in scholarly book publishing. First, a number of academic libraries, some with a university press reporting to it and some without, ventured into the scholarly book publishing sector. While an exciting opportunity for many libraries and presses, this situation is fraught with concerns. Second, a small cluster of university presses was housed within the university library's organizational structure (e.g., Stanford, MIT, Michigan, Temple).

Charles Watkinson, executive director of the University of Michigan Press and also associate university librarian for publishing, which is part of the university's library, has discussed the symbiotic relationship between presses and libraries:

> University presses and academic libraries should be natural allies in the quest to create a more equitable scholarly publishing system. Expert in scholarly information management, situated on university and college campuses, supported to a varying degree by the same funding sources, and sharing many philosophical ideals, librarians and university press publishers seem to be logical partners. . . . There are three main areas of challenge that library/press collaborations face. These are economic, cultural, and structural in nature. . . . Libraries also do not always appreciate that publishing is not a unified activity and consists of many different "publishing fields" with their own values, business models, and ways of doing things; university presses have very different missions and incentives from those of shareholder driven commercial academic publishers.[41]

Watkinson was correct. Academic libraries and university presses housed within a library face a number of issues that must be addressed. It remains to be seen how successful this relationship will be in the coming years. Tyler Walters attempted to analyze future publishing services within libraries,[42] and Heather Moulaison Sandy and Janice Bially Mattern evaluated this relationship, calling it, rather diplomatically, an "evolving art."[43] Kevin S. Hawkins maintained that creating a library publishing program without the benefits of an existing university press creates serious problems regarding launching a program (e.g., books, journals, or both), staffing concerns (e.g., there is a need for acquisition and line editors, skills not commonly found with librarians), and budget issues.[44] Of course, handling art, design, layout, and page make-up; getting a title into the channels of distribution; and processing returns and issuing credits for returns can tax the expertise of seasoned publishers, so it is likely a library would outsource these functions. However, universities facing difficult financial situations might find moving a press into a library an attractive way to keep a press alive and hopefully save some money.

Academic libraries starting a publishing operation de novo without the benefit of an existing university press generates a substantive number of issues. Perhaps the most important issue centers on the issue of "academic prestige." Clearly, a major university without a university press, perhaps California Institute of Technology or Brown University, could address "prestige" issues since they are well-respected higher education institutions. But "academic prestige" is at the heart of hiring, tenure, and promotion procedures, and would an assistant professor up for tenure (perhaps in a history department) with a book published by Brown University, merely for example, be evaluated positively against what has become a traditional template of university press rankings (e.g., Toronto)?[45]

Secondary concerns center on how a library can approach and master the myriad publishing details that a traditional publisher handles: acquisitions, editing, etc. Third, is a library in the publishing sector for the long term or merely as an experiment? Fourth, will the support and funding of a publishing program from a university face the same uncertainties that plague academic programs that fail to generate the expected revenues and/or prestige?

Academia lives in the shadow of prestige, an all-too-elusive "gold standard" of recognition, status, and, for universities, major research grants and gifts from alumni. For academics, the goals are upward mobility toward tenure, full professorships, and endowed chairs. Publishing with a university library could be an exciting opportunity, the "kiss of Lamourette"[46] for a young scholar. Or it might not be the "beginning of a beautiful friendship."[47]

SUMMARY

First, university presses and commercial scholarly publishers are not in the product/book business. They are a business, although university presses are nonprofit businesses, that is, §501(c)(3). Second, you must understand the unique way supply and demand operate in the scholarly communications field. The supply of manuscripts significantly exceeds the ability of every university press and every commercial scholarly publisher to publish all of these manuscripts. And the basic law of supply and demand found in every economics textbook really does work in the constantly changing publishing marketplace.

Third, scholarly publishing is a complex, adaptive, semi-chaotic business with dual-sided uncertainty. In essence, this is a business, because of high book return rates, where no one knows very much for sure, although there are a few exceptions (e.g., *The Chicago Manual of Style* and books by Michael E. Porter, Burton G. Malkiel, Robert J. Shiller, Richard H. Thaler, etc., continue to sell for years and in some instances decades).

Fourth, authors must understand that every university press and commercial scholarly publisher is in a tournament against every other university press and commercial scholarly publisher to acquire and publish the best books that fit into the press's mission and list while, hopefully, generating enough revenues to keep their parent institutions happy and their publishing operations solvent. Fifth, to do this, scholarly publishers traditionally created a diversified portfolio of books, perhaps a strong list of titles in the humanities (e.g., a series on John Milton or the Romantic poets), or, possibly, a book list that addresses regional or state/provincial issues (e.g., the role of female grade-school teachers in 19th-century Texas).

Sixth, some university presses created other revenue streams: some launched third-party distribution operations; others had a strong journals publishing arm that generated revenues to support scholarly books. A few presses had endowments, and some ran bookstores. Some published textbooks. Seventh, what had been a rather cozy scholarly publishing world in the decades before and after the end of World War II changed dramatically with the introduction of expensive scholarly journals (the "serials crisis"); the computer and the internet; e-readers, e-books, and tablets; a very sophisticated online used book market; university endowment shortfalls, library budget shortfalls, and state budget cuts to higher education; increased costs of operating a press (e.g., packaging, printing, and binding; plant), etc.

Eighth, by the 1990s, every university press was in an "arms race" to remain relevant, to compete aggressively in the various channels of distribution, and to understand the shifting scholarly book marketplace. Other substantive issues related to collecting, aggregating, and analyzing incomplete sales information in their business-to-business (known as B-2-B) world. So, the editorial/marketing playing field, while never level, became completely uneven in the early years of the 21st century, and university presses had to compete against prestigious and well-funded trade houses (e.g., Knopf/Penguin Random House, Norton, Basic Books, etc.). Some authors realized that advances (and large ones at that) were also available from trade or commercial scholarly publishing operations (e.g., Elsevier, Kluwer, Sage, Wiley, Routledge/Taylor & Francis, Springer/Palgrave Macmillan, etc.).

Ninth, OA sounds great to many librarians and academics, but there is no free lunch. Printed and digital e-books are expensive to publish. Someone has to pay the costs to publish a book, issues addressed by Maron, Mulhern, Rossman, and Schmelzinger. Tenth, the ubiquitous used book and pirated book websites pose a serious threat to publishers, authors, and the basic concepts of copyright law.

Eleventh, the channels of distribution have shifted, and the traditional terms and conditions of sale, including discount rates, changed in the years since 1990. This poses a challenge to the economic stability of every scholarly book publisher, impacting attendance at scholarly conferences, printed and online catalogs, and the inevitable use of social media to publicize a new season's book list. In addition, there has been a decline in the number of bookstores in the United States. For example, there were 25,137 bookstores in the United States in 2002; by 2017, there were 11,432, a decline of 54.52%.[48] What this does to "discoverability" of scholarly books has yet to be determined, but it cannot be good for scholarly publishers, authors, or society.

Twelfth, consortia sharing of books was accepted by many academic libraries and universities as a way to address budgetary issues; however, some authors, and the Author's Guild, expressed concerns about the impact of book sharing on royalty revenues.

Scholarly books, printed or e-books, will not disappear. But the firm bedrock of traditional scholarly publishing has sustained "business tremors" in recent years, a shifting of the ground under the feet of publishers and authors. Predicting the future has never been easy, but books will prevail as they have since that fateful day when the first book was printed in 1478 at Oxford.

NOTES

1. Allison Schiff and Alex Daniel, "Offset Printing Versus Print-on-Demand," *Publishers Weekly*, https://www.publishersweekly.com/pw/by-topic/authors/pw-select/article/63094-offset-printing-versus-

print-on-demand.html. Also see Paceprint, "General Printing," https://paceprint.ie/lithographic-printing- vs-digital- printing.

2. Ronald C. Jantz, "E-Books and New Library Service Models: An Analysis of the Impact of E-Book Technology on Academic Libraries," *Information Technology and Libraries* 20, 2 (2001): 104–113.
3. Marilyn Deegan, "Academic Books 'At a Crossroad,'" https://www.researchinformation.info/news/academic-books-crossroads. Also see Rebecca Lyons and Samantha Rayner, eds., *The Academic Book of the Future* (New York, London, and Cham, Switzerland: Palgrave Macmillan, 2016), 1–9; Erin Carreiro, "Electronic Books: How Digital Devices and Supplementary New Technologies Are Changing the Face of the Publishing Industry," *Publishing Research Quarterly* 26, 4 (December 2010): 219–235.
4. Hanno Ronte, "The Impact of Technology on Publishing," *Publishing Research Quarterly* 16, 4 (December 2001): 11–22. Also see Yabing Jiang and Evangelos Katsamakas, "Impact of E-Book Technology: Ownership and Market Asymmetries in Digital Transformation," *Electronic Commerce Research and Applications* 9, 5 (September–October 2010): 386–399; Xuemei Tan and Bill Martin, "Digital Technologies for Book Publishing," *Publishing Research Quarterly* 26, 3 (September 2010): 151–167; John D'Ambra, Concepcion S. Wilson, and Shahriar Akter, "Application of the Task-Technology Fit Model to Structure and Evaluate the Adoption of E-Books by Academics," *Journal of the Association for Information Science and Technology* 64, 1: 48–64. https://doi.org/10.1002/asi.22757.
5. Cornell University Library, "Report of the Collection Development Executive Committee Task Force on Print Collection Usage," https://confluence.cornell,edu/display/culcdsc/CUL+collection+use+sudy+%282009-10%29.
6. Rebecca Schroeder, Tom Wright, and Robert Murdoch, "Patron Driven Acquisitions: The Future of Circulation Development?," http://dx.doi.org/10.5703/1288284314834. Also see Karin J. Fulton, "The Rise of Patron-Driven Acquisitions: A Literature Review," http://digitalcommons.kennesaw.edu/glq/vol51/iss3/10.
7. Edward A. Goedeken and Karen G. Lawson, "The Past, Present, and Future of Demand Driven Acquisitions in Academic Libraries," http://lib.dr.iastate.edu/libcat_pubs/60. Also see Stephen Arougheti, "Just-in-Case Versus Just-in-Time: A Paradigm Shift in Collection Development," http://www.ala.org/acrl/publications/keeping_up_with/pda; Online Computer Library Center (OCLC), "Options for Implementing Your Demand Driven Acquisitions (DDA) Program Using the WorldCat Knowledge Base," https://www.oclc/org/content/dam/support/knowledge-base/oclo_dda.pdf.

8. David C. Tyler, Christina D. Falci, Joyce C. Melvin, and Anita M. Kreps, "Patron-Driven Acquisition and Circulation at an Academic Library: Interaction Effects and Circulation Performance of Print Books Acquired via Librarians' Order, Approval Plans, and Patron's Interlibrary Loan Requests," https://digitalcommons.unl.edu/libraryscience/292. Also see Kurt Munson and Hilary H. Thompson, "Giving Your Patrons the World: Barriers to, and the Value of, International Interlibrary Loan," *Libraries and the Academy* 18, 1 (January 2018): 17–34; Joseph J. Esposito, Kizer Walker, and Terry Ehling, "PDA and the University Press," *Journal of Scholarly Publishing* 44, 3 (April 2013): S1–S62; Shane Nackerud, Jan Franseb, Kate Peterson, and Kristen Mastel, "Analyzing Demographics: Assessing Library Use Across Institution," *Libraries and the Academy* 13, 2 (April 2013): 131–145; Michael Levine-Clark, "Access to Everything: Building the Future Academic Library Collection," *Libraries and the Academy* 14, 3 (July 2014): 425–437.
9. William H. Walters, "E-Books in Academic Libraries: Challenges for Acquisition and Collection Management," *Libraries and the Academy* 13, 2 (April 2013): 187–211. Also see William H. Walters, "The Death and Migration of Book Collections in Academic Libraries," *Libraries and the Academy* 18, 3 (2018): 415–422; Stanley M. Besen and Sheila Nataraj Kirby, "Library Demand for E-Books and E-Books Pricing: An Economic Analysis," *Journal of Scholarly Publishing* 45, 2 (January 2014): 128–141; MIT Press, "MIT Press Direct Is the Best Way for Libraries to Offer MIT Press eBooks to Their Patrons," https://direct.mit.edu/books/pages/About?utm_source=ACRL_Newsletter_Feb2019&utm_medium=email&utm_campaign=ACRL_Newsletter_Feb2019&utm_content=MIT_Press_Direct: "Libraries can access the complete collection, with more than 2,500 eBooks and approximately 200 added each year, or subject-specific collections. . . . DRM-free: users can print, copy and paste, and download PDFs by chapter. Unlimited simultaneous users. Consortia discounts available."
10. Jessica Poland, "Electronic Reserves: A Manual and Guide for Library Staff Members," *Libraries and Culture* 40, 2 (Spring 2005): 2002–2003. Also see JoAnn Jacoby and Mary S. Laskowski, "Measurement and Analysis of Electronic Reserve Usage: Toward a New Path in Online Library and Service Assessment," *Libraries and the Academy* 4, 2 (April 2004): 219–232.
11. Anne E. Bromley, "UVA Library, UVA Press Partner to Make Original Scholarship Freely Available," https://news.virgini.edu/content/uva-library-uva-press-partner-make-original-scholarship-freely-available.
12. The National Association of College Stores, "Research," https://www.nacs.org/research.aspx. Also see Erik Brynjolfsson and Michael Smith,

"Frictionless Commerce? A Comparison of Internet and Conventional Retailers," *Management Science* 46, 4 (April 2000): 563–585; Karen Clay, Ramayya Krishnan, and Eric Wolff, "Prices and Price Dispersion on the Web: Evidence From the Online Book Industry," *Journal of Industrial Economics* 49, 4 (December 2001): 521–540; Judith Chevalier and Austan Goolsbee, "Measuring Prices and Price Competition Online: Amazon.com and BarnesandNoble.com," *Quantitative Marketing and Economics* 1, 2 (June 2003): 203–222; James E. Foster and Andrew W. Horowitz, "Complimentarily Yours: Free Examination Copies and Textbook Prices," *International Journal of Industrial Organization* 14, 1 (1996): 85–99; Rubina Vohra, "Rethink the Economics of Textbook Market," *International Journal of Humanities and Social Science Review* 1, 2 (April 2016): 1–6.

13. Supreme Court of the United States, "SUPREME COURT OF THE UNITED STATES Syllabus KIRTSAENG, DBA BLUECHRISTINE99 v. JOHN WILEY & SONS, INC. CERTIORARI TO THE UNITED STATES COURT OF APPEALS FOR THE SECOND CIRCUIT No. 11–697. Argued October 29, 2012—Decided March 19, 2013."

    "Opinion of the Court NOTICE: This opinion is subject to formal revision before publication in the preliminary print of the United States Reports. Readers are requested to notify the Reporter of Decisions, Supreme Court of the United States, Washington, D. C. 20543, of any typographical or other formal errors, in order that corrections may be made before the preliminary print goes to press. SUPREME COURT OF THE UNITED STATES No. 11–697 SUPAP KIRTSAENG, DBA BLUECHRISTINE99, PETITIONER v. JOHN WILEY & SONS, INC. ON WRIT OF CERTIORARI TO THE UNITED STATES COURT OF APPEALS FOR THE SECOND CIRCUIT [March 19, 2013] JUSTICE BREYER delivered the opinion of the Court. . . . We must decide whether the words 'lawfully made under this title' restrict the scope of §109(a)'s 'first sale' doctrine geographically. . . . For these reasons we conclude that the considerations supporting Kirtsaeng's nongeographical interpretation of the words 'lawfully made under this title' are the more persuasive. The judgment of the Court of Appeals is reversed, and the case is remanded for further proceedings consistent with this opinion. It is so ordered."
14. Matthew Jones, "Academic Piracy: Where Next? What Should Academic Publishers Do About eBook Piracy?," *Bookseller*, February 13, 2019, https://www.thebookseller.com/futurebook/academic-piracy-where-next-945416.
15. Judith Rosen, "College Stores Adapt," *Publishers Weekly*, February 18, 2019, http://www.digitalpw.com/digitalpw/20190218/MobilePagedArticle.action?articleId=1464651&app=false#articleId1464651.

16. Association of American Publishers (AAP), "International Copyright Enforcement," https://publishers.org/priorities-positions/international-copyright-enforcement. Over the years, the AAP has worked closely with the US Copyright Office, the US Senate Subcommittee on Intellectual Property, the Committee on the Judiciary, and the Federal Bureau of Investigation. "Intellectual Property Theft/Piracy," https://www.fbi.gov/investigate/white-collar-crime/piracy-ip-theft. The International Intellectual Property Alliance (IIPA), "About," http://www.intellectualpropertyassociation.com/directory/united-states-ip-associations/iipa-international-intellectual-property-alliance: "IIPA—International Intellectual Property Alliance is an Intellectual Property Association located in Washington, United States. Intellectual Property Associations typically provide resources for individuals who are interested in learning more about creating, protecting, or utilizing Intellectual Property. They can also provide introductions or professional networking opportunities for people or businesses who would like to meet professionals who are working in the field of Intellectual Property." Also see Emily Walshe, "The Dark Side of Digitation," *Libraries and the Academy* 7, 4 (October 2007): 491–494; Meredith L. McGill, "Copyright and Intellectual Property: The State of the Discipline," *Book History* 16 (2013): 387–427; Office of the United States Trade Representative, "2018 Special 301 Report," https://ustr.gov/sites/default/files/files/Press/Reports/2018%20Special%20301.pdf: "The Special 301 Report (the Report) is the result of an annual review of the state of intellectual property (IP) protection and enforcement in U.S. trading partners around the world, which the Office of the United States Trade Representative (USTR) conducts pursuant to Section 182 of the Trade Act of 1974, as amended by the Omnibus Trade and Competitiveness Act of 1988, the Uruguay Round Agreements Act, and the Trade Facilitation and Trade Enforcement Act of 2015 (19 U.S.C. § 2242). The Report reflects the resolve of this Administration to call out foreign countries and expose the laws, policies, and practices that fail to provide adequate and effective IP protection and enforcement for U.S. inventors, creators, brands, manufacturers, and service providers. The identification of the countries and IP-related market access barriers in this Report and of steps necessary to address those barriers are a critical component of the Administration's aggressive efforts to defend Americans from harmful IP-related trade barriers. The Report identifies foreign trading partners where IP protection and enforcement has deteriorated or remained at inadequate levels and where U.S. persons who rely on IP protection have difficulty with fair and equitable market access."

17. Digimarc, "E-Book Piracy Costs Publishers $315 Million in Lost Sales," https://www.digimarc.com/about/news-events/press-releases/2017/03/14/e-book-piracy-costs-publishers-$315-million-in-lost-sales.
18. Nielsen and Digimarc, "Inside the Mind of a Book Pirate," https://www.digimarc.com/resources/ebook-piracy-study.
19. Ibid.
20. Imke Reimers, "Can Private Copyright Protection Be Effective? Evidence From Book Publishing," *Journal of Law and Economics* 59, 2 (May 2016): 411–440. Also see Michael D. Smith and Rahul Telang, "Assessing the Academic Literature Regarding the Impact of Media Piracy on Sales," SSRN 2132153 (2012); Martin Zimerman, "E-Books and Piracy: Implications/Issues for Academic Libraries," *New Library World* 112, 1–2 (2011): 67–75; Albert N. Greco, "The Impact of Disruptive and Sustaining Digital Technologies on Scholarly Journals," *Journal of Scholarly Publishing* 48, 1 (October 2016): 17–39; Llkka Kierma, "Commercial Piracy and Intellectual Property Policy," *Journal of Economic Behavior & Organization* 68, 1 (October 2008): 304–318.
21. Association of College and Research Libraries, "Fair Use/Fair Dealing Week," https://www.acrl.ala.org/acrlinsider/archives/17099.
22. Martin T. Buinicki, "Walt Whitman and the Question of Copyright," *American Literary History* 15, 2 (Summer 2003): 248–275. Also see Matthew Redmond, "If Bird or Devil: Meta-Plagiarism in 'The Raven,'" *Edgar Allan Poe Review* 19, 1 (Spring 2018): 88–103; Thomas Owens, "Wordsworth, Galignani, and the Aesthetics of Piracy," *Library: The Transactions of the Bibliographical Society* 12, 1 (March 2011): 23–36; Jason Kolkey, "Mischievous Effects: Bryon and Illegitimate Publication," *Byron Journal* 42, 1 (2014): 21–33; Carrie Sickmann Han, "Pirating Fictions: Ownership and Creativity in Nineteenth Century Popular Culture," *Studies in the Novel* 50, 3 (Fall 2018): 445–447.
23. Nancy Maron, Kimberly Schmelzinger, Christine Mulhern, and Daniel Rossman, "The Costs of Publishing Monographs: Toward a Transparent Methodology," *Journal of Electronic Publishing* 19, 1 (Summer 2016): 4.
24. National Association of Surety Bond Producers, "What Are Surety Bonds?," https://www.nasbp.org/getabond/about-surety/surety-bond: "A surety bond is a promise to be liable for the debt, default, or failure of another. It is a three-party contract by which one party (the surety) guarantees the performance or obligations of a second party (the principal) to a third party (the obligee)." The process starts with a scholarly book publishing firm contacting a surety bond company (the first party), and the publishing firm takes out a surety bond for a certain amount of money (perhaps $50,000), covering any tariff on the importation of books. The surety bond company guarantees that the publishing firm

(the second party) will pay any and all required tariff(s) on the importation of books to the appropriate US government agency (the third party, the obligee). Article 1, Section 8 of the US Constitution states (this article is reproduced as it appears in the Constitution) that: "The Congress shall have Power To lay and collect Taxes, Duties, Imposts and Excises, to pay the Debts and provide for the common Defence and general Welfare of the United States; but all Duties, Imposts and Excises shall be uniform throughout the United States," https://www.archives.gov/founding-docs/constitution-transcript.

25. US International Trade Commission, "The Harmonized Tariff System," https://www.usitc.gov/glossary/term/harmonized-tariff-schedule-united-states-hts: "The Harmonized Tariff System Schedule of the United States (HTS) sets out the tariff rates and statistical categories for all merchandise imported into the United States. The HTS is based on the international Harmonized System, which is the global system of nomenclature applied to most world trade in goods."
26. The author prepared (in 1998 and between 2003 and 2015) the US book exports and imports article for *The Bowker Annual*, which changed its name to *The Library and Book Trade Almanac*. I had annual discussions with several ITA representatives about the monitoring of book exports. I was not able to get any definitive answers regarding the ITA's monitoring.
27. US Internal Revenue Service (IRS), "Tax Information for Charities & Other Non-Profits," https://www.irs.gov/charities-non-profits. Nonprofits are covered by IRS section 501(c)(3): "To be tax-exempt under section 501(c)(3) of the Internal Revenue Code, an organization must be organized and operated exclusively for exempt purposes set forth in section 501(c)(3), and none of its earnings may inure to any private shareholder or individual. In addition, it may not be an **action organization, i.e.,** it may not attempt to influence legislation as a substantial part of its activities and it may not participate in any campaign activity for or against political candidates. Organizations described in section 501(c)(3) are commonly referred to as ***charitable organizations***. Organizations described in section 501(c)(3), other than testing for public safety organizations, are eligible to receive tax-deductible contributions in accordance with Code section 170. The organization must not be organized or operated for the benefit of private interests, and no part of a section 501(c)(3) organization's net earnings may inure to the benefit of any private shareholder or individual. If the organization engages in an excess benefit transaction with a person having substantial influence over the organization, an excise tax may be imposed on the person and any organization managers agreeing to the transaction. Section 501(c)(3) organizations are restricted in how much political and legislative (**lobbying**)

activities they may conduct. For a detailed discussion, see Political and Lobbying Activities. For more information about lobbying activities by charities, see the article Lobbying Issues; for more information about political activities of charities, see the FY-2002 CPE topic Election Year Issues."

28. National Bureau of Economic Research (NBER), "US Business Cycle Expansions and Contractions," https://www.nber.org/cycles.html.
29. National Association of College and University Business Officers (NACUBO), "2018 NACUBO-TIAA Study of Endowments," https://www.nacubo.org/research/2019/nacubo-tiaa-study-of-endowments.
30. Carl Straumshein, "Duquesne Press to Close," https://www.insidehighered.com/news/2017/02/07/duquesne-university-press-shut-down-later-year; Scott Jaschik, "University Press of New England Will Shut Down," https://www.insidehighered.com/news/2018/04/20/university-press-new-england-will-shut-down.
31. Antonia C. Schrader, Alexander Grossman, and Michael Reiche, "Towards a Sustainable Open Access Monograph Publishing Workflow for Academic Institutions," https://www.scienceopenaccess/document_file/85306b42-a39b-40bc-93a8-56c193c592f2/ScienceOpwnPreprint/Towards_sustainable_OA_Workflow_OAHverlag_HTWK-Leipzig-final-pdf.
32. Ellen Collins and Caren Millo, "OAPEN-UK Final Report: A Five-Year Study Into Open Access Monograph Publishing in the Humanities and Social Sciences," http://oapen-uk.jiscebooks.org/files/2016/01/OAPEN-UK-final-report-single-page-view.pdf. Similar concerns about issues confronting the movement toward old OA monographs were analyzed by Ernest Abadal, Candela Olle, and Silvia Redondo, "Open-Access Monographs Published by University Presses in Spain," *El profesional de la informacion* 27, 2(2018): 300–311, https://doi.org/10.3145/epi.2018.mar.o8; Jane Winters, "Open Access 'Seems Such a Seismic Change,'" https://www.researchinformation.info/analysis-opinion/open-access-seems-such-seismic-change.
33. Lindsay McKenzie, "Most Popular Open-Access Monographs," https://www.insidehighereducation.com/news/2018/06/01/most-popular-open-access-monographs?utm_source=Inside+Higher+Ed&utm_campaign=3a3afldb12-DNU_COPY_01&utm_medium=email&utm_term=0_1febc04421-3a3afldb12-197784065&mc_cid=3a3afldb12&mc_eid=d241a9bbcc. Also see Christina Emery's article about BMC: "30 Million Downloads of Open-Access Book Chapters," http://blogs.biomedcentral.com/bmcblog.
34. Martin Paul Eve, *Open Access in the Humanities: Contexts, Controversies, and the Future* (Cambridge: Cambridge University Press, 2014), 130.

Also see Xian Gu, P. K. Kannan, and Liye Ma, "Selling the Premium in Freemium," *Journal of Marketing* 82, 6 (November 2018): 10–27; Francis Pinter, "Open Access for Scholarly Books?," *Publishing Research Quarterly* 28, 3 (September 2012): 183–191.

35. University of California Press, "Luminos Open Access," https://www.ucpress.edu/openaccess. Also see Oxford University Press, "Open Access and Academic Monographs: OUP Supports Open Access," https://global.oup.com/academic/open-access?cc=us&lang=en&; Knowledge Unlatched, "Making Open Access Work," http://www.knowledgeunlatched.org; Allison Mudditt, "Opening the Monograph: Lessons From Luminos," *Journal of Scholarly Publishing* 49, 1 (October 2017): 41–52
36. American Council of Learned Societies, "ACLS Humanities E-Book Joins Mellon Foundation NEH Humanities Open Book Initiative," https://www.acls.org/ACLS-News/ACLS-News/ACLS-Humanities-E-Bool-Joins-Mellon-Foundation-and/?category=publicationsandmedia. Also see the National Endowment for the Humanities, "National Endowment for the Humanities and the Mellon Foundation Announce Grants to Digitize Essential Humanities Books," https://www.neh.gov/news/press-release/2018-04-09-Humanities-Open-Book.
37. Association of University Presses, "AAU-ARL-AUP Presses Open-Access Monograph Publishing Initiative," http://www.aupresses.org/resources/for-authors-a-faculty/oa-monograph-initiative.
38. Association of Research Libraries, "TOME FAQs," https://www.arl.org/focus-areas/scholarly-communication/toward-an-open-monograph-ecosystem=faqs; and Association of Research Libraries, "About TOME," https://www.arl.org/focus-areas/scholarly-communication/toward-an-open-monograph-ecosystem. Also see Association of Research Libraries, "Participating Colleges and Universities," https://www.arl.org/focus-areas/scholarly-communication/toward-an-open-monograph-ecosystem/current-participants; Association of Research Libraries, "Committees, Task Forces & Working Groups," https://www.arl.org/ababout/committes-task-forces-and-working-groups#oa-monograph-publishing.
39. Peter Berkery, "Toward an Open Monograph Ecosystem (TOME) Update," https://www.arl.org/storage/documents/publications/2018/07/31-TOME-TOMEUpdate.pdf.
40. Springer Nature, "The OA Effect: How Does Open Access Affect the Usage of Scholarly Books?," https://media.springernature.com/full/springer-cms/rest/v1/content/15176744/data/v3. Also see Glenn Ellison and Sara Fisher Ellison, "Match Quality, Search, and the Internet Market for

Used Books," NBER Working Paper 24197, http://www.nber.org/papers/w24197.

41. Charles Watkinson, "From Collaboration to Integration: University Presses and Libraries," in *Getting the Word Out: Academic Libraries as Scholarly Publishers*, ed Maria Bonn and Mike Furlough (Chicago: Association of College and Research Libraries, 2015), 83, 95, and 97.
42. Tyler Walters, "The Future Role of Publishing Services in University Libraries," *Libraries and the Academy* 12, 4 (October 2012): 425–454.
43. Heather Moulaison Sandy and Janice Bially Mattern, "Academic Library-Based Publishing: A State of the Evolving Art," *Library Trends* 67, 2 (Fall 20128): 337–357.
44. Kevin S. Hawkins, "Creating a Library Publishing Program for Scholarly Books: Your Options Are Limited," *Journal of Librarianship and Scholarly Communications* 7 (General Issue 2019), https://doi.org/10.7710/2162-3309.2262.
45. SENSE, "2016 Ranking of Academic Publishers," https://research.usp.ac.fj/wp-content/uploads/2013/09/2016-Ranking-of-Academic-Publishers-v1.0.pdf. This ranking separates scholarly book publishers into three categories, with an "A" ranking indicating "refereed book publications published by the world's top publishers." Twenty-four publishers were in the "A" category, including (and listed alphabetically by SENSE) California, Cambridge, Cornell, Harvard, MIT, Oxford, Princeton, and Yale. Unlike scholarly journal rankings, which rely on citation indices, there is no global ranking of scholarly book publishers. SENSE is just one of several rankings; others often concentrate on a specific academic discipline, perhaps sociology or political science.
46. Robert Darnton, *The Kiss of Lamourette: Reflections in Cultural History* (New York: W. W. Norton, 1991), 3–20.
47. A quote from the motion picture *Casablanca* (1943); script by Julius and Philip G. Epstein and Howard Koch, https://www.scripts.com/script/casablanca_57.
48. Dave Bogart, ed., *The Bowker Annual*, 48th ed. (Medford, NJ: Information Today, 2003), 536; andJohn B. Bryans, *Library and Book Trade Almanac*, 63rd ed. (Medford, NJ: Information Today, 2018), 409.

[6]

MANAGING IN TURBULENT TIMES

Toward New Business Strategies in Scholarly Publishing

THE SCHOLARLY PUBLISHING ENVIRONMENT

Faculty members and researchers live and work in a highly structured and in many ways an inflexible world of "publish or perish." To obtain tenure and promotion or research grants, an academic has to produce high-impact scholarly publications, which can vary significantly from one institution to another and from one academic field to another. For example, an assistant professor of economics at a prestigious university could be given a list of (what many believe) are the top 10 journals in the field.[1] Then this assistant professor could be told to publish a number of articles, perhaps 10, to gain tenure and be promoted to an associate professor. More than 10 articles (generally called "papers") could be required for promotion to full professor. An assistant professor in history might be instructed to publish one or two books with a major scholarly publisher (generally a university press; perhaps Oxford, Cambridge, Harvard, Yale, Princeton, or Chicago) to get tenure and promotion to associate professor; and a third or fourth book with a university press could be necessary for promotion to full professor. However, publishing a book with one of the major commercial scholarly publishers can also count, including W. W. Norton, Basic Books, Knopf, or Palgrave Macmillan in the humanities.

Many academics and university and research institutions support the notion of "publish or perish." The system, while not perfect, enables administrators to find out who is productive, and will help increase the prestige of the university or research facility. The end result is a tsunami of scholarly journals and articles, scholarly books, and preprint articles (sometimes called e-prints) that have engulfed the entire research world. In addition to the millions of articles and thousands of scholarly books published annually, as of January 2019, arXiv had 1,502,407 e-prints.[2] According to the International Association of Scientific, Technical, and Medical Publishers: "the annual revenues generated from English-language STM [scientific, technical, and medical] journal publishing are estimated at about $10 billion in 2017. . . . [A]bout 41% of global STM revenues (including non-journal STM products) come from the USA, 27% from Europe/Middle East, 26% from Asia/Pacific, and 6% from the rest of the world," and the average researcher or academic reads 270 journal articles annually; spends about 30 minutes reading the average article, down from 45 to 50 minutes in the 1990s; spends 5 hours reviewing (pro bono) an article for a journal; and reviews 8 articles annually.[3] Scholars in the humanities and the social sciences generally read dozens of book reviews and journal articles, and perhaps more than 12 books annually.

How big are these scholarly publishers? According to Jim Milliot at *Publishers Weekly*, in 2017 the eight largest scholarly publishers (out of a total of 53 publishing firms in the complete table at *Publishers Weekly*) ranged in total gross revenues from $5.6 billion to $412 million (this is the most recent comparative annual data, which *Publishers Weekly* generally releases in the late summer). These totals include revenues for books, journals, and other items. Total revenues for these eight firms in 2017 topped $20.999 billion, up from $18.743 billion in 2016 (+10.74%). RELX dominated the scholarly publishing sector with

$5.609 billion (26.71% of the total revenues for all eight publishers). Sage is a private company, so it is not included in the *Publishers Weekly* table. See Table 6.1 for the data about these publishers.

The public firms in Table 6.1 generate substantial revenues, and they are monitored closely by a number of major financial service companies, especially when quarterly or annual financial reports are released or a conference call is held for analysts.[4] They are often placed in the "media and entertainment" sector or the "media" or "intellectual property" category.[5]

THE BUSINESS OF SCHOLARLY PUBLISHING

It is clear, using any financial metric, that scholarly publishing is a big business. But, as with any industry, there are concerns about the scholarly publishing environment. First, aside from a remarkably small number of exceptionally large, diversified scholarly publishers that have impressive endowments, highly successful scholarly books, or scholarly journal distribution operations, the clear majority of university presses need subsidies from their university. Learned societies rely on income from regional or national meetings and the sale of publications, and libraries have seen their budgets lag behind sharp increases in expenses in the last 25 years.

Second, the vast majority of scholarly publishers in the United States (and also in Canada) lack scale and, in many cases, substantive financial resources to launch and maintain effective institutional publishing operations, although small institutional repositories are possible. The bottom line is clear: most scholarly publishers are trying to defend their existing market share positions with various strategies and structures; some of these strategies are working, and some of them are not. Clearly, most scholarly publishers must modify their basic business model and either acquire scale or, in the case of university presses, learned societies, and libraries involved in publishing activities demonstrate convincingly

Table 6.1 THE LARGEST GLOBAL PUBLISHERS, 2017–2016 (IN MILLIONS OF US DOLLARS)

Global Rank 2017	*Global Rank 2016*	*Publishing Group*	*Parent Company*	*Parent Company Revenues*	
				2017	*2016*
2	2	RELX Group	Reed Elsevier PLC and Reed Elsevier NV (UK, Netherlands, US)	$5,609	$4,864
3	3	Thomson Reuters	The Woodbridge Company (Canada)	$4,941	$4,819
5	5	Wolters Kluwer	Wolters Kluwer (Netherlands)	$3,994	$3.384
8	10	Springer Nature	Holtzbrinck & EQT and GIC Investors (Germany, Sweden)	$1,956	$1,715
10	9	John Wiley	John Wiley & Sons (US)	$1,719	$1,727
16	15	Informa	Informa PLC (UK)	$1,229	$963
17	16	Oxford University Press	Oxford University (UK)	$1,139	$939

Table 6.1 CONTINUED

Global Rank 2017	*Global Rank 2016*	*Publishing Group*	*Parent Company*	*Parent Company Revenues*	
				2017	*2016*
33	36	Cambridge University Press	Cambridge University (UK)	$412	$332
	Grand Total 8 Publishers			$20,999	$18,743

N.B. *Publishers Weekly* ranked the 53 largest global publishers; the rankings listed above represent that publisher's global ranking. All numbers rounded off. These are net publishers' revenues (i.e., gross revenues minus any returns). They exclude other normal business operational expenditures (e.g., taxes, overhead, etc.).

Source: Jim Milliot, *Publishers Weekly*, August 28, 2018, 57–58.

to their home institutions, their authors, and their customers their nonmonetary social worth. Small- to medium-sized commercial scholarly presses must satisfy boards and stockholders.

Third, markets and opportunities for increased revenue, except for STM publishing, which is dominated by large commercial publishers, are declining. Technology for platforms costs money, and many presses will need to pay to use the content distribution platforms of others, whether in direct fees or lower percentage of revenue garnered from sales. With the growing acceptance of gold open access (OA) publishing formats, books, and journals, someone has to pay the book processing charges (BPCs) and APCs. While hope springs eternal, it is unlikely that many federal or state agencies will provide these charges, pushing the payments onto an academic department or a college or university. Otherwise, the faculty member or the researcher pays the charges.

Fourth, every business entity wants realistic answers to basic marketing questions. Who buys? What do they buy? When do they buy? Where do they buy? How do they buy? Why do they buy? Since a high-impact journal is a brand, journal publishers know which library or content aggregator has a contract with the publisher, and brands offer a number of benefits to customers and firms. Since they are valuable intangible assets that need to be managed carefully (e.g., the *American Historical Review*), journal publishers make sure that readers and libraries positively perceive the differences among history journals (in essence, competing brands) in a product category (e.g., US history journals).

The problem centers on scholarly books. While the publisher and the author might be viewed as brands, publishers sell into a business-to-business (B-2-B) channel of distribution, and they really cannot answer many, if any, of the marketing questions listed previously. Compounding this problem is the inexorable fact that book publishers know that the vast majority of scholarly books have a short life cycle, perhaps one or two years. In essence, book sales basically follow a bell curve of early and late sales, leaving a warehouse filled with copies that never sold.[6] The journal publishers, on the other hand, have sales cycles that last decades (e.g., the *Journal of Marketing*, which started in 1936) and, in a few instances, centuries; for example, *Philosophical Transactions*, of the Royal Society, launched in March 1665 by Henry Oldenberg, still has an impressive market share.

Fifth, every scholarly publisher faces severe challenges, including threats to copyright protection;[7] detailed debates about the "fact" that university presses are or are not in a state of decline;[8] the view that academic publishing is the modern version of the "Wild West" and profits of the commercial presses are "excessive" and not jusified;[9] concerns about diversity in the industry;[10] and exactly what impact, if any, revolutionizing "blockchain" journal publishing will have, and at what cost.[11]

THE UNPREDICTABLE WORLD OF SCHOLARLY PUBLISHING

The entire scholarly publishing sector in the United States is witnessing tremendously important tectonic changes. Perhaps the last time publishing saw changes of this magnitude was in the summer of 1945 when Ian Ballantine launched Bantam Books, a mass-market paperback company that significantly changed the availability of content. Bantam Books put *The Great Gatsby* back into print (it was out of print [OP] in 1940, when F. Scott Fitzgerald died) along with other classics; the price of these paperback books was 25 cents. Ballantine witnessed the wartime distribution of 120 million-plus paperbacks to American military personnel,[12] which helped create a consumer market for inexpensive fiction and nonfiction paperbacks when the majority of these 16 million personnel were released from military service after the end of World War II in 1945.

Everyone in the scholarly publishing sector, both university presses and commercial scholarly publishers, has to ask and answer a very simple question. In what could be described as the scholarly publishing version of "musical chairs," who will be left out when the "music" stops playing, when gold OA books and journals become the standard in scholarly communications, and when inevitably new technologies emerge that impact the industry? It is not a question of "if," but of "when." Or, as one "cultural philosopher" put it, "the future is not what it used to be."[13]

University presses and commercial scholarly publishers that publish print and digital books and journals have to face the inexorable challenges that they confront today and plan for the ones they will confront in the future. In essence, all of them must adopt realistic strategies and the structures needed to implement these strategies. But there is no "silver bullet" that will work for hundreds of small, medium, large, and very large university presses and commercial publishers; there is no elegant mathematical formula, rivaling Black-Scholes,[14] that will unlock the mysteries of scholarly publishing;

and there is no hope for a *deus ex machina*. There is only hard work, and an acceptance that there have been, are, and will be substantive differences between the goals and mission of university presses and commercial scholarly publishers. Yet there are a cluster of common threads that bind these publishers.

What follows are a series of suggestive strategies and structures, based on conversations with scholarly publishers since 1985, that different parts of the eclectic scholarly publishing community might find useful in the short term and possibly in the long term.

SCHOLARLY PUBLISHING STRATEGIES

An impressive list of scholars (and a few nonscholars) wrote about the importance of developing a realistic strategy to address a major problem.[15] The most important contemporary strategy author has been Michael E. Porter. In a series of scholarly books and journal articles, Porter crafted strategic ideas emphasizing a number of substantive issues that can be utilized by many scholarly publishing firms.

First, Porter created the "Five Forces" that every firm must confront. They are (1) the threat of new entrants, (2) the bargaining power of suppliers, (3) the bargaining power of buyers, (4) the threat of substitute products or services, and (5) rivalry among existing competitors.[16] Porter wrote that "in coping with the five competitive forces, there are three potentially successful generic strategic approaches to outperforming other firms in an industry: (1) overall cost leadership; (2) differentiation; and (3) focus. Sometimes the firm can successfully pursue more than one [generic strategic] approach as its primary target, though this is rarely possible."[17]

Regarding overall cost leadership, to make this strategy successful, a firm must have

> efficient-scale facilities, vigorous pursuit of cost reductions from experience, tight cost and overhead control, avoidance of marginal customer accounts, and cost minimization in areas like

> R & D [research and development], service, sales force, advertising, and so on. . . . [This strategy] often requires a high relative market share or other advantages, such as favorable access to raw materials.[18]

Clearly, a cost leadership strategy is possible for the large commercial scholarly publishers and a small cluster of the large university presses (e.g., Chicago). This approach is well beyond the capability of the majority of university presses that lack scale and must rely on those "marginal customer accounts" mentioned by Porter.

Porter's theories about differentiation center on the concept of creating a unique value proposition:

> Creating something that is perceived industrywide as being unique. . . . Differentiation, if achieved, is a viable strategy for earning above-average returns in an industry because it creates a defensible position for coping with the five competitive forces. . . . Differentiation provides insulation against competitive rivalry because of brand loyalty by customers and resulting lower sensitivity to price.[19]

This strategy can work for high-impact journals with a strong brand identity (e.g., *Brain Research, Journal of Cardiology, New England Journal of Medicine*) or scholarly books published by major university presses (e.g., MIT's *The Copyright Book*, 6th ed., by William S. Strong).

The last generic strategy is "focus." This strategy focuses

> on a particular buyer group, segment of the product line, or geographical market. . . . Although the low cost and differentiation strategies are aimed at achieving their objectives industrywide, the entire focus strategy is built around serving a particular target. . . . The strategy rests on the premise that the firm is thus able to serve its narrow strategic target more effectively or efficiently than competitors who are competing more broadly.[20]

This strategy can work if a scholarly publishing firm has a clearly defined narrow focus and a marketing mix and appropriate resources to reach an identifiable target, perhaps publishing books only about 19th-century New England poetry or a journal targeting John Milton scholars perhaps.

Porter clearly does not recommend merging two of them into one strategic approach:

> The firm failing to develop its strategy in at least one of the three [generic strategic] directions—a firm that is stuck in the middle—is in an extremely poor strategic situation. . . . The firm stuck in the middle is almost guaranteed low profitability. It either loses the high-volume customers who demand low prices or must bid away its profits to get this business from low-cost firms. Yet it also loses high-margin businesses—the cream—to the firms that are focused on high-margin targets or have achieved differentiation overall. The firm stuck in the middle also probably suffers from a blurred corporate culture.[21]

There are other scholars who have written about strategy, including Henry Mintzberg, Chan Kim, and Renee Maubirgne,[22] but Porter has been very influential for several decades. While Porter outlined in detail his generic strategies, publishers must decide which ones work and which do not. Then these scholarly publishing executives must craft realistic structures to implement the strategy. What follows are some suggestive structures that could be useful.

SCHOLARLY PUBLISHING STRUCTURES

Since no one business strategy can apply across the board for university presses and commercial scholarly publishers, the following is an alphabetical list of structural elements that could be utilized by some, but not all, presses and firms.

Affinity clusters. A small cluster of university presses could create an "affinity" organization, that is, presses either located in the same state (perhaps Penn State, Pittsburgh, and Temple), presses in an "athletic" conference (perhaps the Ivy League), or presses with the same orientation (perhaps Catholic University, Fordham, Georgetown, and Notre Dame). Each press would keep all editorial functions, from acquisitions to line editing, but all "back office" functions (e.g., art, design, layout, production [including using one printer to obtain the best "bulk" deals on printing, paper, binding, warehousing, distribution, etc.], sales and marketing, and financial operations) could be moved to one centralized location agreeable to all of the presses.

In addition, one new key function of the affinity group would be the creation of a consolidated analytics office working with all of the affinity presses, something that the large commercial scholarly publishers have utilized for years. The functions of this operation could include providing essential sales analytical support across all publishing divisions; working closely with a variety of sales teams to provide a data-driven snapshot of the presses' business; creating and maintaining business intelligence solutions and data analytics tools that will provide key insights to evaluate the overall publishing business and marketplace; contributing to the development of new business initiatives by providing analytical support; conducting regular reviews of sales analysis processes; and providing input and recommendations for improvement and efficiency. The data scientist(s) could also obtain reader "sentiment" data and click-through data. In addition, this approach could focus on creating stronger relationships between a real or potential reader and the publisher's content, along with any postreading or purchase feedback, which can help a publisher improve ordering, fulfillment, and the total experience of a reader. This affinity structure failed with the closing of the University Press of New England, but it has worked for certain presses supported by states (e.g., Florida). However, this approach could help a number of small- to medium-sized presses during a time of fiscal questioning of the importance of a university press by some university administrators (e.g., events at Akron). In essence, it maintains the editorial independence and viability of the presses and, hopefully, reduces or at least maintains or minimizes large changes in annual expenditures.

An audiobook program. While some industry analysts predicted the death of the printed book because of the "inevitable" success of e-books, these same "analysts" missed one of the great success stories of the past few years—the emergence of audiobooks as a major market driver. In 2017, audiobooks (mainly downloads and not physical discs) "generated $2.8 billion [in revenues] in the United States . . . an increase of 22.7% over 2016."[23] Regarding global growth potential, "audiobooks continue to be the fastest growing segment of digital publishing."[24] Pew Research reported that about 18% of Americans listened to an audiobook in 2018.[25]

In July 2018, Princeton University Press launched its own audiobook line. Oxford has its Oxford World's Classics Audio Guides:

> Tune in and let our expert editors and translators guide you through some of the greatest literature from around the world. Listen as they talk about the circumstances in which the authors lived, the origins of their writings, and the reasons for their enduring appeal. Whether you want to find out more about your favorite book, have something stimulating to listen to on your iPod, or are a student writing essays, these easy to listen to guides will stimulate, inform, and entertain.[26]

Titles include the works of Jane Austin, Charles Dickens, and John Locke.[27] Clearly, Princeton and Oxford have impressive reputations, and certain assets that few presses can match. But collectively, an affinity group of presses could consider an audiobook operation.

A chapter sales approach, with metadata. All scholarly book publishers could sell or license digital portions of a book, often chapters of books, into domestic and global channels of distribution (e.g., ProQuest).

This provides an intriguing new revenue source with "minimal" costs to the publisher (e.g., credit card fees) since the content is already in a digital format. This is currently an option with Palgrave Macmillan and a few other publishers.

A complete gold OA digital publishing program with APCs and BPCs. Since the journal section in a number of nations accepted the tenets of Plan S (and an understanding that it is likely that Plan S will change the scholarly publishing landscape), and with a movement toward Plan U and Toward an Open Monograph Ecosystem (TOME), presses should consider adopting a complete gold OA publishing structure as quickly and efficiently as possible. Clearly, such a transformation will have dislocation effects on the publishing community, including the loss of revenues from paid subscriptions and the sale of books.

To address these concerns, scholarly journal and book publishers, including nonprofits, should consider charging submission fees for all journal or book submissions, APCs when an article is accepted for publication, and BPCs when a book is accepted for publication. This would achieve three results: (1) generate a new source of revenue to support the publishing operation, (2) address the "free rider" situation in university presses (i.e., when a faculty member or a researcher not affiliated with a university that has a press submits a manuscript), and (3) minimize if not erase the impact of piracy, book rentals, and the burgeoning used book market.

Many high-impact journals already charge APCs and submission fees, often between $50 and $100 or more. If a department or university is willing to spend hundreds if not thousands of dollars to send a faculty member or a researcher to present a paper at a scholarly conference, then a submission of $50 to $250 is not unreasonable; however, individuals from developing nations can request to have all or part of a submission fee waived.

As for BPCs, using the history book costs listed in Chapter 5 as an example ($28,996.74 in 2015), and using historical data and projections from the Congressional Budget Office (CBO) in the Consumer Price Index (CPI, inflation) for 2016 (2.1%), 2017 (2.1%),

2018 (1.9%), and projections for 2019–2022 (1.9%), the cost to publish this history book in 2020, assuming the CBO projections are accurate, would be about $31,983.29. Using the Luminos BPC as an example, a press could charge a BPC in 2020 between $15,000 and $18,000, and the book publisher would have to determine how it would cover the balance. An alternative pricing structure would be for a press to charge the entire amount, which could be paid by an academic department, a college, a university, a funding agency, or the author. In any case, someone (or some group) has to pay since the publishing entity has to cover its expenditures.

Data . Publishers never have access to enough data, and they never have the time to collect, aggregate, and analyze data. At most university presses, the business manager handles data analysis; at the large commercial scholarly publishing firms, a business staff handles this task. But are these operations providing the right data for a publisher tasked with supervising a complex organization? And can a publisher rely exclusively on business information from widely available and reliable newspapers (e.g., *Wall Street Journal, Financial Times*) or magazines (e.g., *Publishers Weekly, Bookseller, Forbes*)? Does a publisher have the time to go to freely available US government databases to get data on inflation, gross domestic product (GDP), consumer spending in specific areas, education, population growth in specific age and gender cohorts, interest rates, etc.?

There are two data sources that collect, aggregate, and analyze vast amounts of data. First, the CBO releases, twice a year, "The Budget and Economic Outlook: 2019 to 2029";[28] the most recent outlook was issued in January 2019. While the CBO's statistical projections out to 2029 are interesting, a publisher would be more interested in the years 2019 to 2023. CBO's projection for the GDP was:

> Real GDP is projected to grow by 2.3% in 2019 and by an average of 1.7% per year from 2020 through 2023. . . . Most of the growth of output in CBO's forecast over the next few years is driven by consumer spending and, to a lesser extent, business and

> residential investment and exports. Compared with the robust pace of output growth in 2018—3.1%, the fastest annual growth since 2005—output growth is projected to slow in 2019. That projected slowdown largely results from an anticipated slowdown in the growth of business fixed investment, as the positive effects of recent tax legislation on investment growth begin to wane, and from a sharp reduction in federal purchases starting in the fourth quarter of 2019 that would occur under current law. From 2020 to 2023, in CBO's projections, slower growth of consumer spending causes output growth to slow further. Recent changes in trade policy, on net, are expected to have a small, negative effect on real output in the next few years.[29]

The second site is *The Statistical Abstract of the United States*.[30] This collection of detailed statistical tables (some population tables cover the years since 1790) from US governmental and nongovernmental sources (along with useful narratives) provides "one-stop" access to detailed historical tables (e.g., the CPI back to 1950) with demographic projections (e.g., population estimates out to 2050). The following is a list of some of the topics in the *Statistical Abstract* of importance to publishers: population; births and deaths; health and nutrition; education; federal government finances and employment; veteran affairs; social insurance and human services; labor force, employment, and earnings; income, expenditures, poverty, and wealth; prices; business enterprise; science and technology; agriculture; energy and utilities; manufactures; wholesale and retail trade; transportation; information and communications; banking, finance, and insurance; arts, recreation, and travel; accommodation, food services, and other services; foreign commerce and aid; and international statistics.

An on-campus publishing education program. This is a relatively inexpensive way to position a university press or a commercial scholarly publisher as an important member of and contributor to the academic and research community. A program could include, for example, a focused series of free presentations for the entire academic community regarding the journal or book publishing value chain; what an editor looks for in a submitted manuscript; peer review processes for journals and books; an overview of the copyright law of the United States and a typical journal and book contract; the economics of publishing, print, digital printing, and distribution; preprints, electronic reserves, and repositories; and OA options including material on APCs and BPCs.

A merger of commercial scholarly presses. Since the end of World War II, there have been a number of major mergers and acquisitions in the commercial sector, including RELX, Wolters Kluwer, John Wiley, and Springer Nature. One of the major commercial scholarly firms could acquire a small independent publishing firm or a nonpublishing operation, and small acquisitions are likely to occur in the future.

However, a large firm acquiring another large firm would generate intense legal scrutiny and require ultimately legal approval from the United States and the European Union (and possibly other nations). This means that the acquiring firm would have to submit detailed documents to the US government stipulating that such a combination would not be a monopoly, which is a "restraint of free trade." Monopolies are against the public policy of the United States because of (1) the Sherman Antitrust Act of 1890—Section 1 of Sherman stated clearly that a restraint of free trade or commerce was against the public policy of the United States, and Section 2 made it a criminal offense for an individual or corporation to be involved in antitrust activities; and (2) the Clayton Act (1914), which augmented the scope of the Sherman Act.[31] These two acts, and the Hart-Scott-Rodino Act and others passed by Congress, are enforced by either the US Department of Justice or the Federal Trade Commission (FTC). The Department of Justice and FTC evaluate "market" and "geographical area"; the "participants" involved in the merger or acquisition; the level of "concentration" before and after the proposed merger or acquisition; and "market shares," which is based on total dollar sales or capacity currently devoted to the relevant market. To do this the Department of Justice and FTC use the Herfindahl-Hirschman Index (HHI) to measure concentration levels in an industry before and after a possible merger and acquisition.[32]

So, while it is possible that two large commercial scholarly firms could enter into a merger or acquisition, it would be an exceptionally difficult undertaking in light of recent concerns in the United States and the European Union (and elsewhere, including Canada) about concentration levels in the technology, media, and publishing sectors.

A merger of the university press into the library. Some, but not all, universities should consider joining the library and university press together to ensure the future of a university press facing certain "economic" issues. This has worked at several dozen institutions (e.g., Purdue, Michigan). Libraries can provide resources and strong alliances to faculty and students, while presses offer expertise that library publishers do not yet have. A number of universities considered this option and abandoned it for a variety of reasons (Catholic University). So, this model might not work for every university with a press.

"Short" scholarly books. Over the centuries, Oxford and Cambridge set the standards for the scholarly publishing of academic monographs, generally long studies of 256 pages (i.e., four signatures of 64 pages each—books are printed in signatures, generally in multiples of 64 pages), and often well beyond 320 pages (i.e., five signatures, with detailed tables, bibliographies, appendices, illustrations, etc.) on a specific topic. This format served the needs of scholars and readers for centuries.

In the past few years, a number of scholarly book publishers, both university presses and commercial firms, have released "short" (sometimes called "brief") print and digital books, generally between 10,000 and 30,000 words, and the content varies significantly from one press to another.[33] These printed books can utilize traditional lithographic printing technologies; that is, increases in the print run decrease the unit manufacturing costs, which is why a print run of 1,000 units has a lower unit manufacturing cost than a run of 500 copies. An option is a print-on-demand (POD) lithographic printing. POD is a process, for both hardcover and paperback books. A publisher works with a printer to customize a book to sell it on a per-order basis under the publisher's name or imprint. POD means the publisher does not pay for the printed book until after the book is sold to a library, distributor, bookstore, website, or reader, so there is no need to print a title in bulk or hold any inventory. In addition, everything after the sale, from printing to shipping, is handled (generally) by the printer. Once a POD system is created, it takes only a few clicks to fulfill an order after the sale.[34] Once major university presses (e.g., Princeton, Stanford, Oxford, Cambridge, etc.) and commercial publishers (e.g., Palgrave Macmillan) began supporting these "shorts," other publishers began to offer short-form scholarly books.[35]

However, the publication of "shorts" received a mixed response. Leonard Cassuto polled senior academics in the United States. While many of these senior professors supported the use and acceptance of "shorts," not every member of academia was "impressed" with "short" scholarly monographs, called a "mini-monograph" by some academics. Cassuto reported that "for graduate students and junior faculty members, though, the question of whether to publish a mini-monograph is more crucial. Put simply, in what ways will these e-books count? Will they help a graduate get hires? How much help will they give an assistant professor seeking reappointment or tenure?"[36] It is likely that the traditionally long monograph will continue in the foreseeable future. But the changing economics of scholarly publishing favor the publication of printed and digital shorts. So, certain portions of the academy might have to change their perception of the mini-monograph.

CONCLUSION

All of these concepts are of great importance in today's constantly shifting business environment. A pivotal issue not addressed completely by Porter in his analyses of various strategies deals with the importance of finding, hiring, nurturing, and keeping top-flight managers to implement strategies.[37] Some organizations have been able to do this for short periods of time, perhaps 5 or 10 years; a small number have achieved this elusive goal for more than a century (e.g., Harvard and Princeton); and only two reached this level of excellence for more than two centuries (e.g., Oxford and Cambridge). But far too many scholarly publishing companies faltered and were acquired because they failed in strategic planning and, in some instances, in this key human relations area (e.g., Lippincott, Pergamon, Garland).

Perhaps publishing managers should evaluate the strategic managerial practices of the Pittsburgh Steelers. Between 1969 and the present, they had three head coaches (i.e., the top team manager: Chuck Noll, 1969–1991; Bill Cowher, 1992–2006; and Mike Tomlin, 2007–present).[38] These three head coaches won six Super Bowls.

Again, thinking about another one of the ideas of the "cultural philosopher," "it gets late early out there."[39] And it is getting late for many scholarly publishers.

NOTES

1. Repec, "IDEAS/RePEc Aggregate Rankings for Journals," https://ideas.repec.org/top/top.journals.all.html. The ranking of the top 10 journals in economics generally includes the following:

    1. *The Quarterly Journal of Economics*, Oxford University Press
    2. *Journal of Political Economy*, University of Chicago Press
    3. *American Economic Review*, American Economic Association
    4. *Econometrica*, Econometric Society
    5. *Journal of Economic Literature*, American Economic Association
    6. *Journal of Financial Economics*, Elsevier
    7. *Review of Economic Studies*, Oxford University Press

8. *Journal of Finance,* American Finance Association
9. *Journal of Economic Growth*, Springer
10. *Journal of Monetary Economics*, Elsevier

2. arXiv, "14 Jan 2019: The Annual Update," http://arxiv.org: "Open access to 1,502,407 e-prints in the fields of physics, mathematics, computer science, quantitative biology, quantitative finance, statistics, electrical engineering and systems science, and economics. arXiv is owned and operated by Cornell University, a private not-for-profit educational institution. arXiv is funded by Cornell University, the Simons Foundation and by the member institutions."
3. Mark Ware and Michael Mabe, *The STM Report: An Overview of Scientific and Scholarly Journal Publishing,* 4th ed. (The Hague, The Netherlands: International Association of Scientific, Technical, and Medical Publishers, 2015), 2; and Rob Johnson, Anthony Watkinson, and Michael Mabe, *The STM Report: An Overview of Scientific and Scholarly Publishing* (The Hague, The Netherlands: International Association of Scientific, Technical, and Medical Publishers, 2018), 3.
4. For example, the following financial service analysts participated in the Wolters Kluwer N.V. Full Year 2018 Results Earnings Conference Call on February 20, 2019: Sami Kassab, Exane BNP Paribas; Matthew John Walker, Credit Suisse; Nick Dempsey, Barclays; Chris Collett, Deutsche Bank; Katherine Tait, Goldman Sachs; and Patrick Wellington, Morgan Stanley. RELX is also followed closely by these same financial firms, and all of these firms issue detailed financial analyses, including projected income of the major firms. For example, the RELX financial notes in 2019 were lengthy, including Morgan Stanley (February 14, 2019, 26 pages); Deutsch Bank (February 12, 2019, 13 pages); and UBS Research (January 17, 2019, 30 pages). Morgan Stanley (https://amr.thomsonone.com/Download.ashx) projected that RELX's STM annual revenues would be +2.4% in 2018; +2.2% in 2019; +2.0% in 2020; and +1.7% in 2021.
5. McKinsey, "Global Media Report," https://www.mckinsey.com/~/media/Mckinsey/Industries/Media%20and%20Entertainment/Our%20Insights/Global%20Media%20Report%202016/GMO%20Report_2016_Indistry%20Overview_v3.ashx. Also see PWC, "Perspectives From the Global Entertainment & Media Outlook 2018–2022," http://www.pwc.com/outlook.
6. During a tour of a consolidated university press warehouse (housing inventory for three university presses) in Rhode Island, the business manager of one of the presses pointed to a specific book title in a bin. He said, "Last year we sold three of those books." To avoid write-offs of a

title that does not sell, most university press and commercial scholarly publishers send out emails announcing a "special sale" to, as they say, "move units" and generate some income. These sales are generally exempt from triggering any royalties for authors.

7. Simba Information, "Threats to Copyright Protections Seen as 'Existential,' According to Simba Information," https://www.prnewwire.com/news=releases/threats-to-copyright-protections-seen-as-existential-according-to-simba-information-300798046.html: "Maria A. Palente, AAP President and CEO, said these [copyright] industries face an 'existential threat to the legal framework on which publishing depends.'"
8. Samuel Cohen, "Scholarly Publishing's Last Stand: When University Presses Close, so Do Our Minds," https://www.chronicle.com/articles/Scholarly-Publishing-s-Last/3243187. Also see Carlos J. Alonso, Cathy N. Davidson, John M. Unsworth, and Lynne Withey, "Crisis and Opportunities: The Future of Scholarly Publishing," ACLS (American Council of Learned Societies) Occasional Paper, No. 57; ISSN 1041-536X, http://publications.acls.org/OP/Occasional_Paper_057_2003.pdf; Scott Sherman, "University Presses Under Fire," https://www.thenation.com/article/university=pressesd-under-fire; Jennifer L. Holberg and Marcy Taylor, "Editors' Introduction: Getting the Profession We Want, or a Few Thoughts on the Crisis in Scholarly Publishing," *Pedagogy* 4, 1 (Winter 2004): 1–7; Margot Harrison, "Weighing the Losses of University Press of New England," https://www.sevendaysvt.com/vermont/weighing=the-losses-of-university-press-of-new-england/Content?oid=24281275; Kyle Siler, "Future Challenges and Opportunities in Academic Publishing," *Canadian Journal of Sociology* 42, 1 (2017): 83–114; Peter Berkery, "University Presses Are Not in Crisis," https://www.publishersweekly.com/pw/by-topic/industry-news/libraries/article/76726-university-presses-are-not-in-crisis,html; Chris Plattsmier, "University Presses Are Thriving, Not Broken," ACLS (American Council of Learned Societies) Humanities E-Book, https://www.humanitiesebook.org/university-presses-are-thriving-not-broken.
9. Craig Lambert, "The 'Wild West' of Academic Publishing," https://www.harvardmagazine.com/2015/01/the-wild-west-of-academic-publishing. Also see Sabine Hossenfelder, "I Can Understand Anger Against Publishers," https://www.researchinformation.info/scholarly-publishing-research-cycle-2018#; Laura McKenna, "The Convoluted Profits of Academic Publishing," https://www.theatlantic.com/education/archive/2015/12/the-convoluted-profits-of-academic-publishing/421047.

10. Nicole Payer, "The Boys Club: Academic Publishing and Barriers of Access," *Structure of the Book Publishing Industry in Canada Pub 371*, Simon Fraser University Digital Library Publishing, http://journals.sfu.ca/courses/index.php/pub371/issue/niew/1. Also see Albert N. Greco, Amy Brand, and Robert M. Wharton, "Demographics of Scholarly Publishing and Communication Professionals," *Learned Publishing* 29, 2 (April 2016): 97–101. This article was based on an international survey in late 2014 and early 2015 of approximately 6,121 scholarly publishing employees in 33 nations. Nicole Benevento, Albert N. Greco, Toniann Pasqueralle, Clara Rodriguez, Francesca Russo, Alana M. Spendley, Kelly Sullivan, Yiming Sun, and Robert M. Wharton, "Who Publishes More Books in U.S. English Departments, Men or Women?," *Publishing Research Quarterly* 33, 4 (December 2017): 357–372; Matthew Flinders, "Understanding Academic Impact: Fear and Failure, Stealth, and Seeds," https://blog.oup.com/2018/08/academic-impact-fear-failure-stealth-seeds.
11. Alexander C. Kafka, "Will Blockchain Revolutionize Scholarly Journal Publishing?," https://www.chronicle.com/article/Will-Blockchain-Revolutionize/245073. Also see a July 12, 2018, NASDAQ article by Antonio Romero, "Academic Publishing Is Big Business, and How Blockchain Can Make a Difference," https://www.nasdaq.com/aspx/stockmarketnewsstoryprint.aspx?storyid=academic-publishing-is-big-business-and-how-blockchain-can-make-a-difference-cm990552.
12. Bill Lucey, "Why It Took so Long for *The Great Gatsby* to Be Considered a Literary Classic," https://www.newspaperalum.com/2013/05/why-it-took-so-long-for-the-great-gatsby-to-be-considered-a-literary-classic.html: "In 1940, before dying of a massive heart attack in a Hollywood apartment at the age of 44, Fitzgerald earned a grand total of $13.13 in royalties." Also see David Thomson, "City of Dreams," https://www.theguardian.com/film/2005/jan/29/classics: "In 1939, the story goes. F. Scott Fitzgerald earned $33.00 from royalties on all of his books." John B. Hench, *Books as Weapons: Propaganda, Publishing, and the Battle for Global Markets in the Era of World War II* (Ithaca, NY, and London: Cornell University Press, 2010), 11–150; and Molly Guptill Manning, *When Books Went to War: The Stories That Helped Us Win World War II* (Boston and New York: Houghton Mifflin Harcourt, 2014), 31–112. While paperback books (often called "dime novels") existed before 1900, Robert de Graff started Pocket Books in 1939; today it is part of Simon & Schuster (which is part of CBS). During World War II, the US government, with the help of the US book industry, distributed 120 million-plus small, lightweight paperback books (that fit into a pocket). When the bulk of the 16 million men and women left military service and returned home, many of them continued to read books, and mainly paperbacks. Book historian

Kenneth C. Davis called this the "paperbacking of America"; see Davis's *Two-Bit Culture: The Paperbacking of America* (Boston: Houghton Mifflin, 1984), 1–55. Also see Louis Menand, "Pulp's Bog Moment," https://www.newyorker.com/magazine/2015/01/05/pulps-big-monent. Robert de Graff's work was immensely important in the history of the book industry in the United States. Although it is the subject of some debate, many, but not all, book historians believe that Ballantine had a "slightly bigger" impact on the "paperbacking of America" than de Graff.

13. Lawrence Berra, "The 50 Greatest Yogi Berra Quotes," https://ftw.usatoday.com/2015/09/the-50-greatest-yogi-berra-quotes.
14. Fischer Black and Myron Scholes, "The Pricing of Options and Corporate Liabilities," https://www.journals.uchicago.edu/doi/10.1086/260062.
15. Perhaps the origins of strategy can be found in early military tactics. For example, see Gaius Julius Caesar, *The Lives of the Caesars—Julius, Augustus, Tiberius, Gaius, and Caligula*, vol. 1., trans. J. C. Rolfe (Cambridge, MA: Harvard University Press, 1914), 177. Ideas regarding laissez-faire were developed by Adam Smith in *The Wealth of Nations* (New York: Bantam Books, 2003), book 1, chapter 1, pp. 8–9; book 1, chapter 7, p. 69; book 1, chapter 10, p. 136; book 4, introduction, p. 459; book 4, chapter 2, pp. 488–489; book 4, chapter 7, p. 667; book 4, chapter 1, part 2, p. 775. The important theory of comparative advantage was developed by David Ricardo in *The Principles of Political Economy and Taxation* (Mineola, NY: Dover Publications, 2004), preface, p. 1; chapter 1, pp. 11, 32; chapter 2, p. 41; chapter 24, p. 220; chapter 32, p. 276. This concept would be developed in more detail by Michael E. Porter. Other important authors in the strategy field include Frederick W. Taylor, *The Principles of Scientific Management* (New York: Harper & Brothers, 1911), 83; Chester Barnard, *The Functions of the Executive* (Cambridge, MA: Harvard University Press, 1938), 82; Peter Drucker, *The Practice of Management* (New York: Harper & Row, 1954), 34–37, 140, 344; Peter Drucker, *Management: Tasks, Responsibilities, Practices* (New York: Harper & Row, 1974), 43, 140; Peter Drucker, "What Makes an Effective Executive," *Harvard Business Review* 82, 6 (June 2004): 59–60; Kenneth R. Andrews, *The Concept of Corporate Strategy* (Homewood, IL: Richard D. Irwin, 1987), 28; Alfred D. Chandler, *Strategy and Structure: Chapters in the History of the American Industrial Enterprise*, p. 78; Theodore Levitt, "Marketing Myopia," *Harvard Business Review* 53, 5 (September–October 1975): 26–27, 27, 38. Andrew Kirkpatrick analyzed the strategic theories of Warren Buffett in *Of Permanent Value: The Story of Warren Buffett*, vol. 2 (New York: McGraw-Hill, 2000), 1615.
16. Michael E. Porter, "The Five Competitive Forces That Shape Strategy," *Harvard Business Review* 86, 1 (January 2008): 79–93. Also see Michael

E. Porter, *Competitive Strategy: Techniques for Analyzing Industries and Competitors* (New York: Free Press, 1998), 1–33; Michael E. Porter, "What Is Strategy?," *Harvard Business Review* 74, 6 (November–December 1996): 70; Michael E. Porter, *Competitive Advantage: Creating and Sustaining Superior Performance* (New York: Free Press, 1998), 4–10, 14–25.

17. Porter, *Competitive Strategy: Techniques for Analyzing Industries and Competitors*, 35.
18. Ibid., 35–36.
19. Ibid., 37–38.
20. Ibid., 38.
21. Ibid., 41–42. Also see Michael E. Porter, *On Competition, Updated and Expanded* (Cambridge, MA: Harvard Business School Press, 2008), 117–154. Also see Joan Magretta, *Understanding Michael Porter: The Essential Guide to Competition and Strategy* (Boston: Harvard Business Review Press, 2012), 43–45, 47–51, 70–71, 114–115. Graham Kenny, "A List of Goals Is Not a Strategy," https://hbr.org/2014/11/a-list-of-goals-is-not-a-strategy.
22. Henry Mintzberg, "The Fall and Rise of Strategic Planning," *Harvard Business Review* 72, 1 (January–February 1994): 107, 113. Also see W. Chan Kim and Renee Maubirgne, "Blue Ocean Strategy," *Harvard Business Review* 82, 10 (October 2004): 76–84.
23. Michael Kozlowski, "Audiobooks Generated $2.8 Billion in 2017," https://goodreader.com/blog/audiobooks/audiobooks-generated-2-8-billion-in-2017.
24. Michael Kozlowski, "Good E-Reader Global Audiobook Report for 2019," https://goodreader.com/blog/audiobooks/good-e-reader-global-audiobook-report-for-2019.
25. Andrew Perrin, "Nearly One-in-Five Americans Now Listen to Audiobooks," http://www.pewresearch.org/fact-tank/2018/03/08/nearly-one-in-five-americans-now-listen-to-audiobooks.
26. Princeton University Press, "Announcing PUP Audio," http://blog.press.princeton.edu/2018/07/09/announcing-princeton-audio. Oxford University Press. "Oxford World's Classics Audio Guide," https://global.oup.com/academic/content/series/o/oxford-worlds-classics-owc/audio-guides/?cc=us&lang=en&.
27. Oxford University Press, "Oxford World's Classics Audio Guides," https://global.oup.com/academic/content/series/o/oxford-worlds-classics-owc/audio-guides/?cc=us&lang=en&.
28. Congressional Budget Office, *The Budget and Economic Outlook: 2019 to 2029* (January 2019), https://www.cbo.gov/publication/54918.
29. Ibid., chapter 2, 21.

30. US Census Bureau, *The Statistical Abstract of the United States*, https://www.census.gov/library/publications/time-series/statistical_abstracts.html.
31. The Sherman Antitrust Act of 1890 is a federal statute that prohibits activities that restrict interstate commerce and competition in the marketplace; https://www.law.cornell.edu/wex/sherman_antitrust_act. The Sherman Act was amended by the Clayton Act in 1914. The Sherman Act is codified in 15 U.S.C. §§1–38, https://www.law.cornell.edu/search/site/clayton%20act. US Department of Justice, Antitrust Division, "Division Manual," https://www.justice.gov/atr/division-manual, last updated April 2018: Introduction; chapter 1, Organization and Functions of the Antitrust Division; chapter 2, Statutory Provisions and Guidelines of the Antitrust Division; chapter 3, Investigation and Case Development; chapter 4, Litigation; chapter 5, Competition Advocacy; chapter 6, Division Resources; chapter 7, Antitrust Division Relationships With Other Agencies and the Public.
32. Association of University Presses, "Short-Form Digital Grows at University Presses," http://www.aupresses.org/news-a-publications/aaup-publocations/the-exchange/the-exchange-archives/summer/2012/800-short-form-publishing.
33. The Hart-Scott-Rodino Act, https://www.ftc.gov/enforcement/premerger-notification-program: "The Hart-Scott-Rodino Act established the federal premerger notification program, which provides the FTC and the Department of Justice with information about large mergers and acquisitions before they occur. The parties to certain proposed transactions must submit premerger notification to the FTC and DOJ. Premerger notification involves completing an HSR Form, also called a 'Notification and Report Form for Certain Mergers and Acquisitions,' with information about each company's business. The parties may not close their deal until the waiting period outlined in the HSR Act has passed, or the government has granted early termination of the waiting period." The Herfindahl-Hirschman Index, https://www.justice.gov/atr/herfindahl-hirschman-index: "The term 'HHI' means the Herfindahl–Hirschman Index, a commonly accepted measure of market concentration. The HHI is calculated by squaring the market share of each firm competing in the market and then summing the resulting numbers. For example, for a market consisting of four firms with shares of 30, 30, 20, and 20 percent, the HHI is 2,600 ($30^2 + 30^2 + 20^2 + 20^2 = 2{,}600$). The HHI takes into account the relative size distribution of the firms in a market. It approaches zero when a market is occupied by a large number of firms of relatively equal size and reaches its maximum of 10,000 points when a market is controlled by a single firm. The HHI

increases both as the number of firms in the market decreases and as the disparity in size between those firms increases. The agencies generally consider markets in which the HHI is between 1,500 and 2,500 points to be moderately concentrated, and consider markets in which the HHI is in excess of 2,500 points to be highly concentrated. *See* U.S. Department of Justice & FTC, *Horizontal Merger Guidelines* § 5.3 (2010). Transactions that increase the HHI by more than 200 points in highly concentrated markets are presumed likely to enhance market power under the *Horizontal Merger Guidelines* issued by the Department of Justice and the Federal Trade Commission. Also see Albert N. Greco, "The Impact of Horizontal Mergers and Acquisitions on Corporate Concentration in the U.S. Book Publishing Industry: 1989–1994," *Journal of Media Economics* 12, 3 (Fall 1999): 165–180. Also see Albert N. Greco, "Mergers and Acquisitions in Publishing, 1984–1988: Some Public Policy Issues," *Book Research Quarterly* 5 (Fall 1989): 25–44.

34. Stanford University Press, "Stanford Briefs," https://www.sup.org/books/imprints/?imprint=STANFORD%20BRIEFS; Oxford University Press, "Very Short Introductions," https://global.oup.com/academic/content/series/v/very-short-introductions-vsl?cc=us&lang=en&; Benedicts Page, "CUP Launches Big Programme of Speedy, Mid-Length Publishing, Cambridge Elements," https://www.thebookseller.com/news/cup-launches-big-programme-speedy-mid-length-publishing-cambridge-elements-933356; Palgrave Macmillan, "Palgrave Pivot," https://www.palgrave.com/us/palgrave-pivot.
35. Georgetown University Press, "Georgetown Shorts," http://press.georgetown.edu/georgetown/a/FOR%20OUR%20AUTHORS/Georgetown%20shorts. Also see Erik Cagle, "Commercial Printing: The Economics of Printing's Evolution," https://www.piworld.com/article/commercial-printing-the-economics-printings-evolution-17233/all; University of Houston, College of Technology, "The History of Lithography," http://sites.tech.uh.edu/digitalmedia/materials/3350/History_of_Litho.pdf.
36. Leonard Cassuto, "The Rise of the Mini-Monograph," https://www.chronicle.com/article/The-Rise-of-the-Mini-Monograph/141007#comments-anchor.
37. Peter Cappelli, "The Mistakes Firms Make With Hiring: They Focus Too Much on Costs, Rather Than Finding the Best Candidates," *Wall Street Journal*, February 25, 2019, R5.
38. The Pittsburgh Steelers, "Pittsburgh Steelers Media Guide 2018," https://www.steelers.com/team/media-guide.
39. Berra, "The 50 Greatest Yogi Berra Quotes," https://ftw.usatoday.com/2015/09/the-50-greatest-yogi-berra-quotes.

INDEX

For the benefit of digital users, indexed terms that span two pages (e.g., 52–53) may, on occasion, appear on only one of those pages.

Tables and figures are indicated by *t* and *f* following the page number

www.ingramcontent.com/pod-product-compliance
Lightning Source LLC
Chambersburg PA
CBHW072127310726
49122CB00004B/248
9780190626235